the Qatar Edge

by

Joey D. Ossian

authorHOUSE™

1663 LIBERTY DRIVE, SUITE 200
BLOOMINGTON, INDIANA 47403
(800) 839-8640
WWW.AUTHORHOUSE.COM

© 2005 Joey D. Ossian. All Rights Reserved.

No part of this book may be reproduced, stored in a retrieval system, or transmitted by any means without the written permission of the author.

First published by AuthorHouse 12/16/04

ISBN: 1-4208-1440-0 (sc)

Library of Congress Control Number: 2004099375

Printed in the United States of America
Bloomington, Indiana

This book is printed on acid-free paper.

Many of the events and situations in this book are true. However, some names of people and places have been changed to protect the privacy of individuals.

Be sure to read these other

authorHOUSE books

from Joey Ossian

Things turn out best for those who make the best of the way things turn out.

- Jack Buck

Foreword

Bad things happen to good people. Clint Eastwood made it popular to think this way: Adapt, improvise, overcome. It applies to many more circumstances than just those that the Marines in the movie, *Heartbreak Ridge*, dealt with. Those bad things become one of two things: Road Blocks or road bumps. Now, I won't pretend to be Dr. Phil or any self-help guru, but it makes a lot of sense to think that we control that outcome.

Road blocks are things we can't get past, putting the brakes on our lives. Road bumps are much more easily navigated and sometimes hardly noticeable, depending on the effectiveness of your personal shock absorbers.

I hit some fair road bumps in the last few years and my entire life from marriage and family to career path have been largely impacted by them. I don't claim to have survived Armageddon, or any other apocalyptic event, I just want to share how I reacted and where it got me today. There is a chance that somebody somewhere may take something from my experience.

I got the title for this book, *the Qatar Edge*, from Thomas A. Edwards, who was deployed with me at Al Udeid Air Base, Qatar. He hails from Colorado Springs, Colorado. Tom suggested the title for its obvious word play. Cutter, or actually cutting, is supposed to come to the reader's mind when they read it. It works well, if the reader knows the correct pronunciation of Qatar. Unfortunately, the American media has not used the correct pronunciation frequently enough that the masses understand the word play just yet. Perhaps this book will help.

I think it's important here to explain why this book is in two parts, and what the connection is between them. Some readers may think I just tossed these two unrelated stories together without thinking. I gave significant thought to how I could explain the connection of my interrupted civilian career to my military deployment. In my mind, they go together, but the more I look at it, the harder it is to see. Perhaps both parts are experiences that will haunt me for the balance. Perhaps my excuse is no better than Bill Murray's in *Stripes*, when he joined the army because his life took a turn for the worse. Here they are, together anyway.

Part One, The End of a Career, isn't just for school teachers or administrators, it's for anyone in a position of authority who has a job where there are risks involved with youth or the other gender. It's for anyone working in a location where you will need witnesses, or someone to back-up your version of the story. My version began as sort of a therapeutic diary. I was being railroaded out of my chosen career (education) by an enemy of my father who decided the best way to get back at him was through me. After you read about the way I was black-balled, you will be convinced that the man is one of those folks who thinks God is just an imaginary friend for adults. As a result of the Professional Practices Commission investigation, I had to respond to some allegations and tell my version of the story. You'll see a fictional version of that ordeal here.

Part Two, the Qatar Edge, isn't just for airmen or even the military. It's for anyone who appreciates good humor under strange circumstances. If you fit both of the suggested categories, I highly recommend the book. It will open your eyes and make you laugh. If you fit one category, read both parts anyway. It won't take long, and you'll be glad you did. At the worst, you'll learn something about the risks in education, and the lighter side of today's military.

The two parts are further related, because without the occurrence of the first I wouldn't have been available for the second, the training/deployment to the Persian Gulf area. I'm not certain if that's clear enough. Perhaps it's partially because of my military frame of mind and commitment to supporting my country. The desire to support my country as a result of 9.11 was strengthened tremendously, and the first time I deployed, I had to be released from the school to participate. Ever since I was a freshman in Ms. Teresa Gabriel's typing class, tapping out that first sentence, "Now is the time for all good men to come to the aid of their country," it's all I ever wanted to do. Freedom is a concept that I believe so strongly in, I wanted to help other countries achieve it as well. The black-balling from the world of education made me look elsewhere, focusing on other things – ok, out of necessity, but nevertheless, it led me to the base where I was a member of the Nebraska Air National Guard. I needed something to do, and I was available. My Group Commander said that appearing eager and "volunteering" to go was strongly encouraged.

Together, the two parts describe a couple years worth of road bumps and how I've adapted, improvised, and overcome.

Joey Ossian in Doha, Qatar. Photo taken by Tony Shimley.

This book is dedicated to the outstanding men and women stationed at Al Udeid Air Base, Qatar, in particular, the 379th Expeditionary Maintenance Group (EMXG). A special thanks goes out to the following folks for providing their leadership and friendship. We made a great team, and I will cherish the memories.

John Stankowski III	David Olson
Anthony Shimley	Thomas Edwards
Katrina 'Kat' Salvesen	Dave Johnson
Rodney 'Dutch' Umbaugh	James Terhardt
Dennis Lockhart	Mike Worthington
Leigh Fields	Molly Erickson
Gabe Sirlopu	Cory Shipp
Father Jose Del Toro	Chaplain Terry Fox
Jeff Decker	Craig Hall
Mike Golden	Frank Faulhaber
Teal Clark	Thurman King
Katherine Lewis	Bethany Glenn
Jim Burton	Tiffany Law
James Wine	Mark Campbell
James Moyer	Joe Wolf

and to my editors, Charlie Washuk, and
my father, Dr. James E. Ossian

Additional thanks go to a brilliant illustrator, my brother, Rick Ossian, for providing the sketch of James Moyer's BMW in the snowstorm. Three people in the entire world can appreciate the accuracy of that drawing. I only hope that nameless farmer gets to see it someday.

part one:

The End of a Career

Guilty until proven innocent.

The world of public education isn't like the rest of the world when it comes to innocence and guilt. You could argue either way whether it is right or not, but what it comes right down to is the protection of the kids. As parents, my wife and I don't want our children to be influenced by anybody whose integrity or credibility is in question. So far, we've been really lucky.

During the school year, students are exposed to adult educators as much or more than their own parents. It's no wonder why parents want the highest of moral beings in front of their kids all day. The problem is there aren't enough of those honorable people who want to expose themselves to the risks involved in teaching. What are those risks you ask? Well, it's no secret that teachers aren't the richest folks out there, and the profession of education has historically been scrutinized and labeled as having "pud classes," and "three months off."

Joey D. Ossian

The most dangerous risk in education today, from my perspective, is the risk of being accused of doing something to a student. It's dangerous because for some reason the burden of proof is on the teacher. The media has heightened our awareness of sexual abuse on all fronts, but no environment is more closely watched than our school classrooms. Don't misunderstand. I don't see a problem with that. You never know when another Mary Kay Letourneau is going to turn up. The degree of interaction is high, so the degree of observation should be as well.

What people seem to forget when these incidents get reported is that children have the ability to be creative and manipulative or slant their side of the story when it suits or benefits them. It is human nature to trust a trustworthy person who has earned it over years of being an honorable individual. It is also human nature to doubt a habitual liar who has developed a pattern of deception. Why is it when allegations fly in the face of educators, those norms are discarded? All of a sudden, nobody considers the character of the individuals involved.

My story is not unique. I've heard the countless nightmares from educators that started in the lecture halls at the university. In many cases, all it takes is one accusation, and the career you worked so hard at is over. I hope you have a back-up plan. Guilty or innocent? Read on and decide for yourself.

the Qatar Edge

When I got close to graduation in the Spring of 2000 with a Master's Degree in Educational Administration, I still had no intention of changing positions. My continued pursuit was motivated by greed. More credits would move me on the salary scale. I loved teaching second grade, and was planning on retiring doing just that.

One day, shortly after my fourth knee surgery, I was in the middle of a physical therapy session when I was informed that the K-12 principal at our neighboring school had resigned. Here is my chance, I thought to myself. I won't have to pack up and move, Dad will be pleased that I appear to be following in his footsteps, and my wife won't be displeased with the substantial increase in salary. I updated my resume and threw my name in the proverbial hat. If the worst happened, and I didn't like the job, I could always return to teaching.

Hoping to get some positive kudos and encouragement, I made my intentions known to my father. To my surprise, he told me that I didn't want that job and he warned me about the integrity (or lack thereof) of the current superintendent. I normally took my father's advice and, in hindsight, I should have. When I first met Steve Goracke, I must admit, I was impressed. He appeared confident, intelligent, accomplished, and at ease with himself. Steve made me comfortable immediately. Human beings tend to like people who like them, and in that mind-set, I am no different from the norm. Steve liked me (or appeared to) instantly, and I him. He praised my credentials and made me feel like I had a real shot at being chosen the next Principal of the Buffalo Flats Public Schools. Steve even claimed to admire my father. The following week, prior to the final round of interviews, I toured the building with the school secretary, a woman who would work for me if I was hired. Sharon Smith was older than me, but very attractive. She had an appearance that was friendly, but you could tell her motherly instincts commanded respect from the students. Sharon's approval was crucial, and I was extremely fortunate in this case. I hadn't put it together before because "married status" changed the names. Her mother was a board member at my current school district, and she thought the world of me. I was, as they say, a shoo-in.

The excitement overcame me, and all my father's warnings fell on deaf ears. He knew I would take the job when offered. I wish he would have knocked me over the head with a brick. Dad knew what I was in for, but neither of us could have imagined the depths of the treachery to come.

My first year in Buffalo Flats was a dream come true. I felt I had landed the perfect job. The teachers respected me, the students trusted me, and my rookie year was turning out

the Qatar Edge

to be a huge success. I busied myself with night classes to finish my endorsements, and privately celebrated making the right decision. Little did I know, "Father really does know best."

My second year appeared to be starting off as well as the first, until a Tuesday morning in September. I called my father to wish him a happy 63rd birthday, and he asked me if I was near a television. I turned it on and saw what looked like a 747 Air Bus drive through one of the World Trade Center towers. All I could think of at the moment was when and where will I be going with my Air National Guard unit. I didn't know at the time, but this historical incident and my pending deployment was the first bit of ammunition that Steve needed to build the snowball.

Six months after 9.11, my deployment began. I was off to war, and it was splattered all over the local papers. Guessing is the best I could do regarding what happened at school while I was away. I won't go in to the details of my first deployment against terrorism, because what happened there has little or nothing to do with my career in education, only its demise. My return occurred six weeks later when I discovered that the world as I knew it had changed dramatically. For starters, the school board wanted to meet with me about a few issues prior to my return to work. I soon found out that I was being relieved of my coaching assignments and the board wanted me to hear it from them. Apparently, word had gotten out, and they feared that I would be told through other channels. Confidentiality wasn't a priority to a few of the board members' spouses who were made privy to the information before me.

My suspicion prompted me to request a contract for next year, and I spoke up about the need to renegotiate my salary to compensate for lost wages that went along with the coaching positions. Being put off until July further raised my suspicions. I demanded the "negotiations" be put on the July agenda.

The snowball gets a nudge.

This portion of the book began in the form of notes shortly after I resigned and signed a contract to teach again in another district. I learned from Mr. Ron Schell of the Platte Center Grade School that I was not going to be a teacher in his school as I'd previously thought. The notes I wrote were originally intended to be sent to the Professional Practices Commission as a response to the rumors, a denial of the primary allegation, written material to be submitted with the investigation documents, and an accurate description of the real truth regarding an alleged sexual harassment incident. The writing became a form of therapy for me, and is now intended to serve further in that regard.

the Qatar Edge

Let me begin with some brief background regarding my educational career. My father had been in education for as long as I could remember. My older brother Rick became a teacher of English and art at the high school level. Angie, my only sister, became an elementary teacher toward the end of my duty. My career in education spanned ten years. I began by teaching and coaching in Prairie View in the fall of 1992. I taught third grade for two years, during the 1992-93, and 1993-94 school years. The administration then requested that I move to second grade, due to changing enrollment numbers. I taught second grade from the 1994-95 school year until I finished my Masters in Educational Administration at the University of Nebraska at Kearney at the end of the 1999-00 school year. Then I signed a contract with the Buffalo Flats Public Schools to be their K-12 Principal.

Prairie View sent me off with quite a stack of positive evaluations, and I left on fantastic terms with the staff, students, and community. The relationships I developed with many families and former students in the Prairie View area continue to this day. In fact, several Prairie View students exercised their right to option enroll to Buffalo Flats because of the positive influence I had contributed to their lives.

Joey D. Ossian

From July 2000 through March 2002, I had a glowing record and a positive evaluation as the Principal at BFPS. The community, staff, and students supported me. I frequently heard positive comments regarding my performance from all contingents of the community, including the school board and the superintendent. Sainthood isn't in my future, but I was not aware of any documented negatives to this point.

In mid-March, I received military orders and was required to temporarily leave my position as K-12 Principal at BFPS to deploy with my Nebraska Air National Guard unit, the 155th Air Refueling Wing, to Southwest Europe in support of Operation Enduring Freedom. The desire to deploy and defend my country made me appear excited and anxious and the school board may have misinterpreted this as being happy about leaving them and the school. When Todd Johnson, the board president, caught me grinning while talking about the deployment, I had mixed emotions. I was so stoked about the chance I may get to participate, but slightly embarrassed over what I was willing to sacrifice. Board members probably wondered further if my preparation and thought processes lead to my distraction and perhaps hampered my performance of duties. A co-worker and friend confided in me that I appeared to be giving more thought to my deployment than to my job. Hindsight being 20-20, I can see where this may have happened.

the Qatar Edge

Before my departure, to my surprise, an assembly was held at school. A going away party was thrown in my honor. Many tears were shed. My interim replacement was Ms. Beverly Clay. She was the school counselor at that time, but she held a K-6 administrative endorsement. Bev would make a fitting replacement. During my stay in Southwest Europe, I was the maintenance officer of a composite maintenance squadron including units from the New Hampshire Air National Guard, the Wisconsin Air National Guard, and my unit, the Nebraska Air National Guard. We were tasked with maintaining the KC-135R refueling aircraft during their mission of refueling fighters and bombers on their way to Southwest Asia. The Buffalo Flats School Board received a letter from my group commander that praised my performance. I continued to work for BFPS by email. I worked many issues, and actually did some handbook revision. The Superintendent, Mr. Steve Goracke, requested that I attempt to supplement the social studies curriculum by sending back occasional stories and photos regarding my activities and whereabouts. I told him I'd try, as long as it didn't compromise the unit's security by releasing classified information. Much to the pleasure of my social studies teachers, I believe I exceeded that request beyond their wildest dreams by providing almost daily messages and digital photos.

Joey D. Ossian

My return to Nebraska came at the end of April, on Monday morning the 29th. I was absent for almost seven weeks. The superintendent gave me a mandatory three-day vacation upon my return. I wasn't even allowed to come to the annual awards night on Tuesday evening the 30th of April to present my athletes with their awards (I head coached two varsity sports). I wasn't allowed to come to town to coach my own daughter and her 12-and-under girls' softball team. I wasn't allowed to be seen in town to even show my face until after the superintendent and selected school board members, President Todd Johnson, and my close friend Vice-President Howard Lawson, had a chance to speak with me.

At that Wednesday morning meeting on May 1st, I was informed that I would no longer coach anything at BFPS. The excuse was that I'd be able to spend more time focusing on my primary role of principal. I'm not sure how that information, with little other, warranted being banned from town until the following morning, my first day back at work,

Thursday, May 2nd.

Things went from bad to worse. I got the feeling they were angry at having missed the April 15th deadline to non-renew my contract. Imagine a public education

the Qatar Edge

system non-renewing someone while they are defending their country overseas. Even they knew better than that. Even then, I contemplated resigning and wondered if the superintendent and the school board were attempting to get my resignation.

On a day shortly following, the date escapes me for the moment, but it was in May, Superintendent Goracke and Board President Johnson came to my office. Todd read a two-page list of items I was being blamed for. I was not given the list, nor was I allowed to see it. It had lots of bogus stuff on it from the losing record of the football team (that I DID NOT coach) to leaving school to drive a bus for a kindergarten field trip. The board president claimed I only went because my daughter was one of the kindergartners attending (I was the only substitute bus driver available). Mr. Johnson also accused me to my face of sleeping with my secretary, Mrs. Sharon Smith. That May, I did send out several resumes, only to be talked out of leaving by my superintendent and Board Vice-President, Howard Lawson. Both of them independently made it clear they wanted me to stay.

July 15th, 2002

I attended the scheduled monthly school board meeting in the Family Consumer Science room at BFPS. Vice-

President Howard Lawson was not present at the meeting until approximately midnight. From the beginning of the meeting (7:30 pm) up until about 11:00pm, things went very smoothly. I gave my principal's report that included some things I was working on for recruiting purposes, and I anticipated the coming executive session to be a renegotiation of my principal's contract. Board members asked if I had any input, so I told them I was aware that the teachers would be asked to take a base salary freeze in light of the recently passed levy override. I volunteered to take the same, if I could get the other end of the teacher's deal, vertical movement for the year and horizontal movement for nine credits if achieved. If they could do that, I wouldn't even complain about the loss in pay I'd take from losing the coaching positions. They said they would consider it, and that they would send someone to get me in about 15 minutes.

At approximately midnight, an hour after they began the executive session, Steve Goracke came to my office to get me. He said, "They're ready for you, bye, I'm going home." I was a little surprised that he wasn't going back with me, but I dismissed it because I was exhausted and it was so late. I didn't expect what I went back to. It turned out to be a "Lion's Den" of sorts, and I was the sacrificed lamb. I sat down to hear that I wasn't getting a raise. Then

the Qatar Edge

I learned that the board planned to officially inform me in November that my contract wouldn't be renewed after this coming year. You could have knocked me over with a feather. Of course I asked why, and they claimed that they were doing some reorganization that didn't include me. I asked if that meant they'd combine the counselor and principal positions to save money. They said no. I asked if that meant they would have Steve, the superintendent, run the school from Lincoln, and just appoint head teachers. They said no. They didn't have a reason, they just knew it wouldn't include me. I really began to wonder at this point, what was the point of staying at Buffalo Flats any longer. At roughly midnight, Vice-President Howard Lawson walked into the meeting as President Todd Johnson asked me what I understood from this meeting. I stated that I felt I should finish my course work, polish my resume, and begin job hunting, because it sounded like I wasn't wanted. I added that if we would have had this meeting in May, the board would probably already have my replacement secured. At that point the President began to wrap up the meeting, fairly well signifying that my summation was correct. Howard's jaw almost hit the floor. He appeared to know nothing about what had just taken place.

Todd Johnson approached me immediately after the meeting and asked me what I was going to do, meaning would I send out resumes again, or give them the year as their principal. I told him I'd stay, but privately thought that only because there wasn't much time to go job hunting. Shock had overcome me for the moment. Still, I was not offered a contract.

July 16th, 2002

At 5:00am, with very little sleep, I thought about the events of the previous evening. I drove back to Kearney where I was taking a 7:00am summer class in pursuit of my specialist degree. My father, Dr. James Ossian, and I had a lengthy conversation about the entire ordeal and, with tremendous anxiety, I decided to resign. He assisted me with composing the resignation.

July 17th, 2002

I turned in my resignation on Wednesday, the 17th of July with an ulcer building. I hadn't been unemployed since I was about 14, and didn't like the feeling. With a date of the 17th of July at the top, I made the resignation effective the 30th of June. I personally handed it to Board President Todd Johnson, in an upstairs room of his house at approximately 5:00pm. He was in the middle of a do-it-yourself project. Todd asked me if I was sure this was what I wanted to do, and I assured him it was. I provided him with two signed

the Qatar Edge

copies of the resignation. He said he'd take care of getting a copy to Steve Goracke. I told him I'd clean out my office and turn in the keys within a couple days. My desire to avoid seeing anybody or having somebody see me was so strong, it took me only a few hours to pack and leave.

July 18th, 2002

Because I had no job, I began looking for employment. I did so by sending out email to connections I had made over the last few years. While several positions were brought to my attention, including multiple options in Lincoln, one in Elk Grove, and one in Sand River, I chose to pursue one in Platte Center, NE because of the nature of the position and the proximity to my home.

July 19th, 2002

BFPS sent a paycheck to my home, so I naturally deposited it to my checking account, incorrectly thinking it was compensation for the month of June. I promptly received, via registered mail, notification from Mr. Goracke that I must return the check because it was compensation for July. Since my resignation was effective June 30th, I didn't rate compensation for July. I agreed and reimbursed the school immediately. Also included in the letter was a request that I return the laptop computer that I thought, as

I had noted in my resignation, was compensation for my employment. Since I didn't have it in writing that the laptop belonged to me, I promptly returned it as well.

July 26th, 2002

Mr. Ron Schell of the Platte Center Grade School interviewed me on Saturday, July 20th, 2002, and I was offered a position via cell phone on Thursday the 25th at approximately 8:00am. I signed the contract to teach seventh grade English and science at approximately 10:00am on Friday the 26th of July. The board president and secretary had already signed the contract. I breathed a sigh of relief. I had a job.

August 4th, 2002

I returned home after a weekend drill meeting with the Nebraska Air National Guard on the 3rd and 4th of August. My wife and I and our three children left for vacation. We traveled north that Sunday evening on the 4th, and stayed over night in Yankton, SD.

August 5th, 2002

The following morning we traveled to Sioux Falls, SD. We spent the day shopping and swimming and generally

the Qatar Edge

exploring the sights of the falls in the downtown area. I took many photos that I still think are postcard worthy.

That evening, at approximately 7:00pm, on the way back from the Wild West Family Fun Center, I received a phone call from Mr. Ron Schell, the Platte Center Grade School Principal. He asked if I was in a place to talk about something serious. Curiosity overwhelmed me, but I told him I was driving in bumper-to-bumper traffic and that I'd call him back as soon as I was in such a place. After a drive-through, and a quick trip to the hotel, I returned his call.

Ron told me he received an anonymous, unsigned (they usually are) letter about me that prompted him to call Mr. Todd Johnson, the Buffalo Flats Public Schools Board President. Todd would make no comment, but gave Ron a number at which he could reach Mr. Steve Goracke, the BFPS Superintendent. Ron told me that Steve informed him during that phone call that he had personally filed an ethics complaint with the Professional Practices Commission against me. Ron further informed me that he felt obligated to inform his Superintendent, Mr. Jim Fredenburg, and his school board of these recent developments. Additionally, he informed me that his board was now going to have an emergency meeting on Tuesday, the 6th of August at noon (it just happened to be my 8th wedding anniversary) to decide whether or not to rescind their contract offer to me.

Joey D. Ossian

August 6th, 2002 – Happy Anniversary!

My wife and I decided that the circumstances suggested a return home from vacation earlier than planned, and we arrived home at approximately 2:00pm on the 6th of August. I immediately called Mr. Don Anders of the Professional Practices Commission at the recommendation of my father. Don confirmed that Steve had filed a complaint, but that the Commissioner hadn't yet reviewed it. Don claimed that when the Commissioner reviewed the allegations, I would receive notice of his decision and a copy of the complaint in the mail later that week. At that time, I would be allowed to write a statement supplying further information that I felt would benefit the investigation should one occur.

I called the office of Mr. John Recknor, a lawyer and long time family friend, and left a message with his secretary. Somehow, I felt the need to retain his services. Mr. Ron Schell was next on my short list of phone calls to make. Finding out exactly what the Platte Center school board decided to do during their emergency board meeting was on my agenda. They did rescind my contract. Once again, I became unemployed.

In hindsight, my mind shouldn't have been so boggled trying to come up with a reason for all of this. When I first returned from the deployment, I wondered why things appeared different. I had the feeling that the board and superintendent might want me to leave purely out of fear that

the Qatar Edge

I may be deployed again. While my replacement Bev Clay performed admirably, things didn't run as smoothly in my absence as they had hoped. She was just stretched too thin. I think, maybe, they wanted someone in the position that wouldn't be called away to war again, and that possibility still existed.

The continuation of Steve chasing something baffled me. When I thought all he wanted was my resignation, I gave it to him. When that clearly upset him and the board, it looked like mixed messages. The Board President Todd Johnson actually asked me if I was sure I wanted to resign, and asked me to reconsider.

I'm certain you can now understand my confusion and shock at the current circumstances. The only thing that was clear to me was that Steve wanted my certificate. Why he wanted it so bad will forever remain a mystery to me. From my perspective, Steve's fabrication will deter other districts from employing me in the future anyway, so I may as well frame the certificate and mail it to him, so he can hang it above his fireplace.

August 10th, 2002, Saturday morning, from the National Guard base in Lincoln, NE.

Thursday, the 8th of August, my wife called to inform me that we had received notification that registered mail needed to be picked up at the post office in Prairie View (10 minute drive from our place). She asked if I wanted her to get it, and would I come home to read it, anticipating that it was from the Department of Education, and the Commissioner's office. At her recommendation, I remained in Lincoln, and she picked up the envelope on Friday morning. I opened it when I arrived home that evening at approximately 5:00pm. One glance at the allegations of inappropriate student contact almost made me vomit, so I put it away for further reading on the morning of Saturday, August 10th, 2002.

The reason that this complaint/allegation seems possible is that it is based on some, but very few facts. Let me begin with some background regarding my relationship with the students whom Mr. Goracke had spoken with.

Stacy, an 18-year-old student at BFPS, was previously a Prairie View student. She chose to option enroll to Buffalo Flats, if memory serves correctly, at the beginning of her junior year. She wasn't one of the students I mentioned previously that I'd come to know in Prairie View, but from my perspective, we were quickly becoming friends at the same level I viewed those other students. I frequently counseled her on issues that typical teenagers are involved with to include, but not limited to: boys, alcohol, drugs, and sex. I'd say we had a good principal/student relationship, and I kept many discussions to myself when it involved

the Qatar Edge

things for which she could get into trouble. Had I been a better friend and principal, I would have advised her more strongly to avoid such behaviors.

Amy, a 19-year-old graduate of the Prairie View Public Schools, was never one of my students. She was a Buffalo Flats resident who chose to option enroll to Prairie View (quite the reverse from the norm) in order to participate in softball, which wasn't offered by the Buffalo Flats Public Schools. I do know her, however, because of my relationship with her parents and her sister, Samantha, a Buffalo Flats student. I'll include a major incident in this report involving Amy's family here, because I feel it may be important to establish a possible motive for Amy.

During the basketball season of this past school year, Samantha and another student reported to practice. It was brought to my attention by another player that she suspected Samantha and her friend might be under the influence of something illegal. I talked to the coach, Mr. Steve Cooper, and told him I would hang around to investigate, and see what I thought. I determined that Samantha and her friend might possibly be drunk. I felt this way because Samantha has the reputation of being a heavy drinker, and her appearance showed that she was sluggish, had bloodshot eyes, and was just plain not her normal sober self. I confronted her first, and she denied any wrongdoing. Then I confronted the other involved student. The second student quickly admitted that she and Samantha smoked marijuana while riding around in a car with a boy before coming to basketball practice. Since the second student implicated Samantha, I then confronted Samantha again, and this time she confessed to the same behavior.

I immediately phoned the parents to come speak with me. Samantha's father, a local farmer, came to my office to discuss the matter. Samantha again, confessed to the wrong doing in the presence of her father and admitted that she lied to me when I first asked. At that point, I was very lenient. Subconsciously, that may have been because I was a friend of the family. She received a suspension from school (five days if I remember correctly), and was removed from the basketball team. Samantha was a sophomore, and a valuable member of the junior varsity squad. She also filled in considerable time with the varsity squad. The coach, wasn't happy, but supported me in this decision, because he helped write and adopt the activity policy.

The following day, Samantha's father claimed that Samantha never confessed. I incorrectly assumed that his integrity would allow me time to get a signed confession, but it didn't. The punishment stuck, however. Prior to this incident, I considered that family to be my friends. That probably is no longer the case. Within the week, Samantha's

the Qatar Edge

mother, resigned her position as art teacher for the school. This incident may or may not have given her daughter Amy some motive to say negative things regarding me.

If I kept a list of all the students I'd been a friend to, or another list of students that I'd ticked off, I'd never get to my real job, because in the principal's role, you would add several names to both lists on a daily basis. I have lost count of the number of times I have been alone with female students. In fact, I've probably gotten to the point where my sensitivity is dulled to how dangerous that environment could be to my career. For the last two years, I've driven multiple students to Rotary luncheons, physicals, and therapy appointments, just to name a few. Some of those trips were as far as Lincoln, and more often than not, I was alone with a female student. I chaperoned many school dances, and even danced with girls when they asked. I even posed for a yearbook photo to appear as if I was dancing with a male student as a joke. I supervised events where students were working on school activities after school hours. If I had a character flaw in this area of behavior, you would think it would have come out before now.

The facts to my knowledge regarding the allegations are as follows:

I did have many email and MSN (instant messenger) conversations with Stacy. I also had brief phone conversations when she called my cell phone, but I don't recall ever calling her. We discussed many activities in which she was involved. In fact, I kept to myself that Stacy contacted me via MSN from inside the school during school hours. This was obviously inappropriate student behavior, and further inappropriate behavior from me by not enforcing the rules about students not being allowed to participate in such behavior on school computers during school hours. At that time, I thought it was harmless teenage fun.

Stacy wanted me to hook her up with a National Guardsman. I knew I could do this very easily, and I also knew it was wrong, but I felt sorry for her because she wasn't having much luck with the boys in Buffalo Flats. My intention wasn't to create an environment in which she could have sexual relations with someone. I simply wanted to set her up with a nice guy. A nice gesture, yes, but I agree, inappropriate and not within the job description of the principal. I've never had sexual relations, nor intentions of such with Stacy.

Pieces of evidence that are missing are MSN or email conversations where Stacy made very suggestive comments to me. In fact, at one time her sign-in name was "what would you say if I wanted to…" instead of the "god Amy, i hate you!!!lol" that normally was listed. I don't know if this would help me build an entrapment case, or help my

the Qatar Edge

defense at all. I'm not a computer guru, and don't have the time to find those conversations, if they can be found. Even if I knew how and had time, I'm not sure I'd waste it looking for them. In this manner, Stacy frequently attempted to tease and hit on me, but I never hit on her, and I can't see where she got the impression that I did.

In the complaint before the Commissioner, there are further facts and fabrications. Other than the people mentioned and their identities, the facts are the following:

I was in a hotel room (I don't recall the room number) at the Day's Inn (Airport) on June 6th. I continued my stay there through Sunday morning, the 9th, at which time I checked out.

On the evening of the 6th of June, Stacy and Amy called and arranged to meet me outside of the hotel, and both of them accompanied me to my room. You might say this is the point at which my dulled sensitivities came into play. I discovered that they both had beer with them, and were very obviously under the influence of something else, or just a tremendous amount of alcohol. The mistakes I made to this point were multiple, but the worst were (1) allowing them into my room and (2) not calling their parents to report their condition, as appropriate action from an administrator would call for. However, it was summer and off campus and I had no legal obligation to do so.

Joey D. Ossian

I assumed that the girls wanted to talk about something, as we frequently had done, but I had the sense to not visit long. Amy said something about needing a smoke and departed. Stacy stayed for about two minutes, and said she had better leave as well. She left. I did not kiss Stacy, and I did not touch her thigh, as stated in the allegations. There was no "hitting on" from either of us. Stacy simply claimed that she had to be back at some dorm on campus before they were locked out, and left. I was very concerned with their condition, and didn't want them driving anywhere alone but, again, my lack of good judgment didn't move me to call their parents.

August 19th, 2002, Monday morning, from the National Guard base in Lincoln, NE.

I had a wonderful weekend. I spent time with my wife and children, mostly at home. Sunday the 18th had potential to be stressful. My plan was to take a drive with the family over to Columbus, stop at the Hy-Vee tent sale, and then head to Fremont, with a stop at Platte Center. The stop in Platte Center was brief. My wife drove me to the home of Mr. Ron Schell, the Platte Center Grade School Principal. I had a very nice visit with Ron in his front yard, while my family patiently looked on from the family mini-van. The purpose of the visit was to return the building/room

the Qatar Edge

key that had previously been issued to me, along with a few textbooks, and an annual yearbook. Ron and I spoke very comfortably for about 15-20 minutes about a variety of things, but mostly the situation at hand. We parted on good terms, and he asked that I stay in touch and ask for help if I needed it. After a quick lunch at the local McDonald's, we left Platte Center, and headed east for Fremont.

The first stop, and what turned out to be the only stop we made in Fremont, was the Super Wal-Mart. My wife relayed the following story to me regarding what happened there:

While we were in the store (Wal-Mart), between 2:00 and 2:30 pm, my wife was approached by Ms. Julie Finster, the Family Consumer Science teacher at BFPS. Before my wife began the story, I was a little apprehensive because Stacy has a history of frequent contact with Ms. Finster to the point where Stacy sees her as a close friend and confidant. My concern was that Ms. Finster had been convinced to side-up with Stacy and would be filling my wife's head with further fabrications. Quite the opposite was true. Ms. Finster relayed to my wife that she was absolutely appalled at what was being done to me. She further claimed that Stacy had not contacted her once since this story began unraveling. She suspects that Stacy quit calling her because she knew she'd tell her it's a bunch of baloney. Ms. Finster then told my wife that Steve Goracke had been trying to get information out of her, asking for any little thing that might be seen as sexual harassment. When Ms. Finster told him, "No, there isn't anything," Steve then implied a threat by telling Ms. Finster that there is a rumor going around that all she does in FCS class is bake cakes and throw parties.

Some people would say that my judgment throughout this ordeal involving Stacy had not been good, but I don't think I broke any laws. I don't know the laws and rules well enough to know what disciplinary action, if any, that possible lack of judgment merits. The immediate punishments being set before me as I see it are multiple and more than I deserve. I've lost a contract with the Platte Center Grade School. I will not be employed by any school entity this year. My wife is unhappy with the circumstances. These events have caused us both tremendous grief. My children are exposed to a very stressed situation. My wonderful reputation is damaged beyond repair in the community that once embraced me. I'm certain that the Professional Practices Commission may have further punishment (in the form of disciplinary action) in mind for me as well, up to and possibly including the revocation of my teaching certificate. Even the newspapers are calling. They've printed vague stories that connect my resignation and the allegations, and that the board had to approve my resignation because I was under contract. That

the Qatar Edge

simply isn't true. If the incidents are connected, it's because the superintendent is falsely accusing me of things because he is angry that I resigned three weeks before school started. I'd like to see them produce the contract that they say I've signed. It doesn't exist. They never offered me one.

August 22, 2002, Thursday morning

My wife called me at work this morning in tears. The rumors are getting the better of her. Now the word going around Prairie View is that Stacy is pregnant. You'll never guess who they are saying the father is.

With my family supporting me, I decided to challenge the allegations. My lawyer told me that, without proof, I would be found not-guilty. This was the point at which Steve Goracke played his trump card. Seven months into the investigation an allegation was added to the charges. Steve brought to the table an incident that occurred a year prior to my resignation, in my first year as principal. I had attended a conference basketball coach's meeting with three other coaches. A 12-pack was consumed on the way home, provoking us to play a harmless prank on my good friend Howard Lawson, the School Board Vice-President. It was a pay-back prank, because Howard had recently pasted beer labels all over my windshield. My wife saw him stumble out of his truck in the middle of the night. Board members and auto mechanics don't need certificates to do what they do, and they wouldn't be in jeopardy of losing them if they did. We left some beer cans in his yard, and I used a window marker to make a comment on the windshield of his car. The comment said, "Hi Dad," and I signed it with the name of his daughter's boyfriend. Steve knew I couldn't deny the incident, because the following morning, when Howard made the discovery, I was the second phone call he made. Before I could tell him it was a harmless prank, he had made a report to the police.

John Recknor, my lawyer, told me I could still fight this out, but the PPC would find me guilty of the "beer can" incident. I'd spend up to $10,000 getting the misconduct allegations removed from the charges, and lose the case because I did throw the beer cans. John recommended that I deny, but plead no contest to the original allegations, and plead guilty to the most recent developments. It was taking a chance, but John thought the PPC would recommend no more than two years suspension of my teacher's certificate. The commissioner's final ruling was five years. My career in education was essentially over. In fact, I don't know if I can ever bring myself to teach in the future. There would always be that fear that somebody could do this to me again. I never want to go through it again, and I couldn't put my family through it. I guess the important thing is to not lose the lessons or the humbling feeling. Unfortunately, the worst feeling is never hearing a "thank-you" or anything from the other guilty coaches for whom I took the entire rap. I can't say I blame them. After all, they have their own families and careers to be concerned with.

part two:
the Qatar Edge

A portion of the Persian Gulf area. In the center is the peninsula country, Qatar, the location of the largest coalition Air Force in history.

My air-conditioned tent, located in Camp Andy at Al Udeid Air Base, Qatar.

How all this Al Udeid stuff started.

In the summer of 2003, I was a sucking up some active duty days at the hangar, still job hunting and working on part II of *A Marine's Lapse in Synapse*, when I got some interesting email traffic. The Air Force needed somebody to fill a slot at Baghdad International Airport (BIAP) with my Air Force Specialty Code (AFSC). The traffic came my way, because they knew I was available, and they were leaning toward "inviting" me. I felt the need to make a contribution, but mostly, I needed a job. Mr. Michael Hanf, from Langley Air Force Base, appeared to be the originator of the message, so I contacted him via email. His organization does all the placement of core personnel and they wanted an experienced Captain for the position as an Executive Officer in a Maintenance Group. I wasn't a Captain, and I had no experience in a group headquarters. My "bio" began with "I have no experience as an Exec, since I just graduated from BCOT (Basic Communication and Information Management Officer Training) in Biloxi this spring. I'll be eligible for Captain before the arrive NLT (no later than) date," and it ended with "but I have 20 yrs experience in MX (Maintenance)." I thought that my lack of rank and exec experience would cause Mr. Hanf to move onto the next person on the list. Mr. Hanf's reply was "you're just what we're looking for," so the wheels got motion.

"Volunteering" for Baghdad got a few strange reactions from my colleagues, family, and friends. I tried to explain that what looked like volunteering wasn't really what it appeared. When you're asked if you're available for a deployment, what they mean is, if you don't have wedding, funeral, or birth-of-a-child plans pending, you're available to go. I began the process of out-processing, which involved multiple shots to prepare for diseases we don't worry about in the U.S., and an issue of uniforms, boots, flack vest, and chemical protection gear, which would help me blend into (and be protected from) the environment. I was feeling a curious combination of excitement and anxiety, when a week before my planned departure, I was informed that my final destination would not be the Baghdad International Airport. My Unit Deployment Manager (UDM) informed me that shortly after a drop off in Bahrain, I'd be getting

the Qatar Edge

off in the Connecticut-sized peninsula country of Qatar. I had never heard of the place, and I had no idea where it was located. Consulting the map, I learned that it was across the Gulf from Kuwait, bordering Saudi Arabia, and very near the United Arab Emirates.

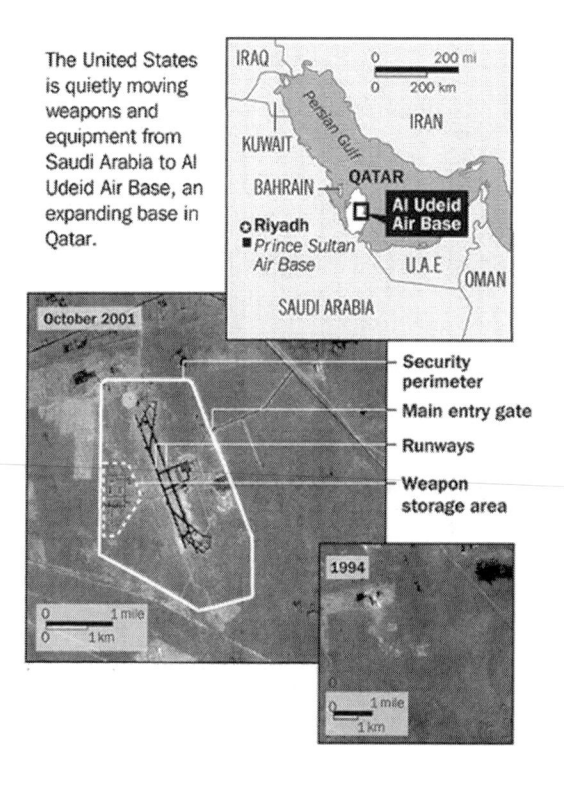

The United States is quietly moving weapons and equipment from Saudi Arabia to Al Udeid Air Base, an expanding base in Qatar.

- Security perimeter
- Main entry gate
- Runways
- Weapon storage area

October 2001

1994

I heard from some of the more senior maintainers that there was a base in Qatar inheriting all the equipment left over from Prince Sultan Air Base (PSAB) in Saudi Arabia.

I have to admit here, that I was initially disappointed that, although I'd be close, I probably wouldn't get a chance to see Baghdad. I'm not a terribly religious man, but the desire to see the region of the Tigris and the Euphrates, where life itself is alleged to have begun, was strong. The UDM assured me that just because my primary location was Qatar, didn't mean that I'd remain there for the duration. I had the opportunity to fly to Iraq a couple times, so I have seen it in person, but my time there was negligible compared to many of my military counterparts.

The impact on my family was another story all together. Staci was 12 and, unfortunately, she might have been privately celebrating my departure. She and I were having a rough time dealing with her pending teenage needs. Samantha took it the worst. She was eight at the time, and just beginning to understand the concepts of global distance, time in months, and war (as much as an eight-year-old girl can). Sammy was, and still is, Daddy's girl. Carter was three and a half when I left, and he had no idea what was about to happen. He had no concept of where I was going or for how long. Carter was used to me attending Guard drills, so Mommy told him I went to Guards.

Qatar

Ruled by the Al Thani family since the mid-1800s, Qatar transformed itself from a poor British protectorate into an independent state with significant oil and natural gas revenues. During the late 1980s and early 1990s, the Qatari economy was crippled by a continuous siphoning of petroleum revenues by the Amir, who had ruled the country since 1972. He was overthrown by his son, the current Amir Hamad bin Khalifa Al Thani, in a bloodless coup in 1995. In 2001, Qatar resolved its longstanding border disputes with both Bahrain and Saudi Arabia. Oil and natural gas revenues enable Qatar to have a per capita income not far below the leading industrial countries of Western Europe.

Of the 800,000 people who live in Qatar, only 200,000 of them are indigenous to the peninsula. The others come for work from small countries like Nepal and the Philippines, or from the military coalition: The United States, The United Kingdom, Australia, and Singapore.

I was picked up at the Doha International Airport late on the evening of March 14th by two of my future co-workers. SSgt James Terhardt and 2Lt Leigh Fields were standing in a crowd looking for a man they had never seen, holding a sign with my name on it (that they couldn't pronounce). Had I acted any more like a tourist, I would have missed it, and probably had to call a cab. I looked around to get my bearings, and my name on the sign caught my eye. The trip back to base from the airport should have told me that driving in this country was an "every man for himself" experience, but I was too busy taking in the scenery and visiting with my new co-workers to notice the poor driving habits of the locals.

Arriving at the base was my first taste of real base security and a search-pit. We were after curfew (but safe with the excuse of picking me up), so the search area wasn't crowded. Roughly six or eight groups of people had to exit their vehicles and sit in a wooden shack-like enclosure with no windows, while the security police and their dogs searched through the contents of the vehicles. The wait wasn't long, but we passed the time getting to know each other a little. I was exhausted, thinking only of sleep. James and Leigh seemed to pick up on this, so they gave me the

the Qatar Edge

option of a drive-by at the base "choke and puke" (grab 'n' go/flight kitchen) prior to depositing me and my luggage in my new home for the next 125 days. We'd get all the visiting we wanted over the next several weeks.

I lived in an air-conditioned tent, only a block away from the nearest Cadillac (nicer version of restroom/shower). The first two months the circuit breaker always had to be reset for the lights to work and, until I figured out the best time of day to take one, my "combat" (three-minute limit) showers were always cold. I had a grey metal wall locker, a two-level plywood bookshelf, inscribed by its builder with a black Sharpie, and a welded tube metal bunk, too short for my 6'2" frame. Some kind soul left me a replica of a "magic carpet" that covered a 3' x 5' area of my section, and I shoved all my duffel bags under the bunk. Once you got used to the roar of the jets at all hours of the night, you only had to put up with the wind snapping the flaps and loose parts of the tent. My "Alaskan" style tent housed six people, all of whom were Executive Officers for one of the organizations on base. I'm not sure why we were grouped together unless somebody thought we'd swap creative ideas in the middle of the night. It was one of the few co-ed tents on base, having four males and two females for most of my time. I lived in a corner, so my only common plywood divider was shared with Captain Kathy Lewinsky. She was raised in small town Nebraska, just an hour from me, but we had to travel half way around the world to meet. I thought it odd that she so frequently had a late night male visitor until she introduced me to her husband Carl, who was fortunate to be deployed to the same location as his wife. Separation pay was automatic. I wonder if they went to any trouble to point out to their administrative sections that they didn't rate it.

I started out thinking I'd have to spend my days at the Sun Spot, a back-yard type, above ground pool that usually turned out to be the dude-fest. I definitely wasn't going to fit into any of the desert queen entourages. I'm married, and it was just too comical watching the young men fall into them. Each female was waited on, hand and foot, by about four to six guys, each thinking they would be the "chosen one" to get a sniff. If one did get lucky, they'd have to find a hiding place in one of the bomb bunkers where there was always a disgustingly large collection of used condoms. One fact remains about women. It doesn't matter what you look like, it's all about what else is available.

My new friends, James and Leigh were packing and preparing to leave when I arrived. I was Leigh's replacement, and James would be replaced shortly after her departure. Getting to know them was bitter sweet, because I knew they would only be around long enough for me to start liking them.

the Qatar Edge

James was training me to be an off-base driver's trainer. The training consisted of showing me around the capital city of Doha, and discussing defensive tactics to avoid colliding with the locals who weren't required to have a license or any sort of training at all. Their only requirement to drive was to have possession of an automobile with the appropriate keys. Doha ranks right up there with the worst driving conditions on earth. Not only do they not have any training required, but the rapidly developing country hasn't had any motorized form of transportation except for the last few decades. Three lanes of traffic frequently had four and five cars side by side. Navigating the detours, construction, roundabouts and abandoned/wrecked vehicles was more "experiencing" than anything. That left James and I time to talk and tell stories. He is the only person alive to ever ask me to repeat stories. James would laugh time and time again, and every time he would introduce me to somebody, he would ask me to tell them a story. Needless to say, James's love for my stories caused me to enjoy his company. James and I spent quite a bit of time together. Thanksgiving was upon us, and we were both going to miss being with our families. I'm secure enough in my manhood to say that James is the most handsome sumbitch I've ever seen.

Joey D. Ossian

James Terhardt and I spent Thanksgiving in Al Udeid with Lakenheath troops.

Following 2Lt Fields was going to be challenging. She was a former high school math teacher turned motivated young officer trying to keep herself busy by starting multiple projects. I'm a "git-r-done" type of officer, but I don't take on too much at once. Unfortunately, 2Lt Fields left me with a few of her unfinished projects. Don't misunderstand, she had no intention of burying me with work. It was no fault of hers, the materials just hadn't arrived on time for her to complete the job herself. A week after her departure, the shed arrived. James was still on board, but his replacement, Gabe Sirlopu, had arrived. The three of us planned to take on the shed construction project. The directions that came with the box claimed that two people could finish the project

the Qatar Edge

in three hours. After the three of us had five hours invested, we were at the point of exhaustion where everything done and said was hilarious. My primary duty was holding things in place while reading the directions. We were joined by Chief Tony Shimley and MSgt Mike Worthington. With their help over the next two hours, we completed the shed.

Joey Ossian, Gabe Sirlopu, James Terhardt, Tony Shimley, and Mike Worthington pose in front of the completed shed project.

Mike Worthington was from Lakenheath Air Base, England. My connection with Mike was mostly talking about how much we missed our wives and the kinky fantasies we hoped to live out when we returned to our respective homes.

Like much of the aircraft maintenance, the picnic table project was awaiting parts. Fields's intention was to provide a place to sit for all the new troops waiting for transportation at the pax (passenger) terminal. The lumber had arrived before her departure, and she showed me where it was stored across from the Armament Shop. We were waiting on the hardware.

Just enough time had passed that I had forgotten about the picnic table project. People leaving, replacements getting up to speed, and the transition of taking over the group office staff was enough for the time being. When the bolts showed up, I put it off until new folks were comfortable. The first task of re-locating the lumber proved to be a stumbling block. My sense of direction was just good enough to have found the place where 2Lt Fields had previously taken me. Tom Edwards was the NCOIC of the Armament shop. We were becoming fast friends, but had only met that week. Tom knew of the lumber, but didn't know it was ear-marked for anything. When asked about the wood-pile by the Australian Maintenance crews next door, he told them he didn't know either, and they accepted that as "up for grabs." My picnic table lumber became an Australian gazebo. Tom and I managed to soak them for a few beers in exchange for "forgetting" about the lumber. I could have dropped the project right there, but I was trying to make a good impression on the Colonel. I approached him about the problem. The Colonel said the project was actually the Wing Chaplains' Group, and that 2Lt Fields

the Qatar Edge

was just assisting them. If I wanted more guidance on it, I should talk to the Maintenance Group Chaplain. Captain Terry Fox was the current chaplain assigned to us and he had an office in our building. The chaplain was rarely there, due to his duties at the base Chapel, so I began to compose an email. I attempted to be funny, making numerous references to "wood," and did the Chaplain know anything about "wood." The email humor was lost except for the Bcc: including Chief Shimley. Chaplain Fox claimed to know nothing about the project. James went back to Hill Air Force Base in Utah, and to my knowledge, picnic tables were never built.

It didn't take long before I was welcomed into a group that mixed some of my co-workers and their friends. Most nights, the group would attempt to plan a get together. That event usually involved watching episodes of season one and two of *The Shield* with Michael Chicklis if everybody could be there. If not, we'd pick a movie that usually took half the night to agree on.

Chief Master Sergeant Anthony (Tony) Shimley was the Wing Weapons Manager, and the center of the group. He was raised on Bazooka Bubble Gum in Duryea, PA. (18642). Chief was the connection that brought us together. Tony has a magnetic personality and a sincere approach to life that just makes you want to be his friend. He achieved the rank of Chief Master Sergeant (E-9) early in his career, and everybody knew that great things were expected of him. Hanging around with the Chief frequently reminded me of the military jargon that I had forgotten. His only hang-up was being late for our social events. We knew it wasn't his fault, but we gave him crap about it anyway. Chief always had to stop and visit with people. Everybody knew him, and always had an issue with which to bend his ear.

Thomas Edwards was the Non-Commissioned Officer in Charge (NCOIC) of the Armament Shop. Like me, he may have been a "Shimley follower" but he is also a true leader in every sense of the word, inspiring his troops to perform above and beyond the call at every opportunity. Tom is truly "tip of the spear." We had a connection from day one. When Tom first walked into my office, late November of 2003, my email announcement went off. "What's your name, Scumbag?" We were in mid-conversation, but he stopped when hearing R. Lee Irmey's voice, not sure if he heard what he thought he'd just heard. He turned to look at me. "Am I hearing things?" "That's my email." "That's what mine says too." From that moment on, Tom and I discovered many other things we had in common. Tom still claims the best thing he took home from the deployment was a cardstock certificate I made up for him. The S.H.A.T. (Shit

Hot Armament Troop) certificate was a close replica of the certificates prepared for the Airman of the Month awards, and I slipped it into the pile for the Colonel's signature. The Colonel either signed it without knowing he did, or saw it, thought it was deserved, and signed it anyway.

Tony Shimley and Tom Edwards posing with their toys.

Katrina Salvesen slipped into our group in the strangest way. Kat was the first female C-130 Loadmaster in the history of The Royal Australian Air Force. It so happened that Chief Shimley and Major Teal Clark from the AMXS (Aircraft Maintenance Squadron) had flown to Iraq for a site survey in order to see if a runway was usable. Their return trip required travel by C-130, and the one they tried and ultimately successfully boarded just happened to belong to the Aussies and was "owned" by Kat. It was purely another day in her office and it didn't matter how amiable in his negotiations the Chief was. She wasn't about to just let anybody board her aircraft.

Katrina 'Kat' Salvesen, the first female C-130 Loadmaster in the history of The Royal Australian Air Force.

Dave Johnson and I knew each other from Keesler Air Force Base in Biloxi, Mississippi, where we co-coached the over-30 men's basketball team. He was permanent party, meaning he had to be in place for a year. Like many of us, Dave had a cushy-job, so the year was likely to be tougher on his wife and kids.

Rodney "Dutch" Umbaugh called me from the Mesirah Islands a day before he was to arrive in Qatar. Not to arrange for me to pick him up at the pax terminal or to ensure there was a tent space for him, but to introduce himself, and to see if there was anything I needed from his current location. I was very impressed at his professionalism, and made a note to myself to perform in this manner prior to my next relocation. Dutch and I co-founded the FLAG jogging club. The acronym stood for Fat Lazy Aging Guy (or Gal to be politically correct). It eventually became FLAB or Fat Lazy Aging Bastards. We had access to an electronic base bulletin board, where we posted the first meeting of the club. After a couple days, Dave Johnson joined, making us three. A few weeks after that, Dutch had to go home on emergency leave, leaving Dave and I to continue. We faithfully ran at least five nights a week even participating in the President's Day run. We tried every night, but at times, the blowing sand was just too much.

Dutch Umbaugh flying a kite over Camp Andy.

Where were you when . . . ?

We've all heard older generations talk about where they were when John F. Kennedy was assassinated, or how they mourned when they learned that Elvis, The King of Rock 'n' Roll, had passed. I was roughly a month shy of conception when the former President was slain in November of 1963, and again, a month shy of being a teenager when the King over-dosed on August 16th, 1977.

In more recent years, when historical events occurred and the media made those events more memorable, people have attempted to remember where they were and what they were doing, just so they can have a story to tell when people ask.

September 11th, 2001, when the hi-jacked aircraft flew into the Twin Towers in New York City, and the Pentagon in Washington, D.C., or December 13th, 2003, when Saddam Hussein was captured will be significant events to talk about in this manner for years to come. When 9.11 occurred, I was in my office at the Buffalo Flats Public Schools, in Buffalo Flats, Nebraska, where I worked as the K-12 Principal. On that day, I comforted students, and privately wondered where my National Guard unit might get deployed.

I was having this very discussion with a few of my co-workers one night, Wednesday, the 17th of December, 2003, just four days after the capture of the former Iraqi President, Saddam Hussein.

Some background is required regarding our location at that time. We were stationed at Al Udeid, Air Base, Qatar. Most people don't know where the country of Qatar is located. It's a Connecticut-sized peninsula country that borders Saudi Arabia and sticks out into the Southern portion of the Persian Gulf, resting between S.A. and the U.A.E (United Arab Emirates). I worked with a great crew of active duty folks in the 379th Expeditionary Maintenance Group. I was the only Nebraska National Guardsman in the organization, but served just as proudly as the active duty folks while we supported operations in Afghanistan, the Horn of Africa, and Iraq. Our debate started when we talked about what we were doing when Saddam Hussein was captured or what we were doing when his capture was reported. The argument was over who had the worst truthful answer to those related questions.

For the sake of argument and clarification of the related questions, Saddam was captured on Saturday, the 13th of

the Qatar Edge

December, at about 2030 hours (8:30 pm), Iraq time (same as in Qatar). Back home in Nebraska, that's 11:30 am, and I would be having lunch. When his capture was reported, it was Sunday the 14th, at roughly 1400 hours. Folks in the states probably didn't hear about it until they woke up Sunday morning to get ready for church.

The Wing Weapons Manager, Chief Anthony Shimley, a bomb-loader by trade, claimed he had the worst answer, and of course, TSgt Rodney Dutch Umbaugh, public affairs for most of his career, agreed because his answer was the same. We were 20-minutes away from Al Udeid, at the Army base, As Sayliyah, not far from Doha, the capital and most populated city in Qatar. They had a nice facility in which you could work out, get a haircut and an Orange Julius, sit and watch a movie, or other niceties that weren't available in our tent city (affectionately known as Camp Andy) just yet. Their answer to the question, "What were you doing *when you heard* Saddam was captured?" is quite interesting, and not very manly. When the news flash came across the screen, they were both sitting in easy chairs, getting manicures! MSgt Thomas Edwards, the local Armament Flight Chief, wanted to see what all the hub-bub was about, and went for the big screen from his spot at one of the Nautilus bench machines, while I watched the entire televised special from the stirrups of the elliptical jogging apparatus. The manliest answer at that point was definitely Tom's, "I was lifting weights."

I still think my answer to a slightly different, but related question, "What were you doing *when* Saddam was captured?" was by far, more embarrassing than theirs, but we'll let you be the judge. I guess it's all in your perspective. The night before we were informed of the number one towel-head's capture, at the time when it was actually happening, I was involved in a highly covert operation that has remained confidential until this writing. It was Saturday night at the Wagon Wheel (Al Udeid's night-life hot spot), and I was on stage taking my turn at singing on Karaoke night. Confederate Railroad's "Trashy Women" never sounded better. Just a few hundred miles away from Hussein's hometown, I was getting a standing ovation, and chants of "Joey, Joey" could be heard across the compound, while the 4th Infantry Division was dragging Saddam's butt out of a spider hole.

Of course, years from now, when my children and grandchildren ask, or when my co-workers and friends ask, my answer will be, "That's classified." Edwards will probably stick to the real truth when he's asked, but Shimley and Umbaugh have agreed with me that it really wouldn't be a lie if our answer was, "Our commander has advised us not to give out that information."

I wouldn't take a million dollars for any one of my children....but I wouldn't give you a nickel for another.

- Joyce Jacobs

The Deployed Vasectomy

In late December, 2003, I worked for two Colonels in the 379th Expeditionary Maintenance Group, United States Air Force, Al Udeid AB, Qatar. It was a Monday, the 29th of December. The Group Commander, Colonel John F. Stankowski III, had just returned from leave in the states the night before. Dutch Umbaugh and I picked him up at Doha international airport. Lieutenant Colonel David P. Olson, the deputy, was getting ready to take leave. Dutch and I would take him to the airport later that evening. Because of the proximity of the leave schedules, and the simplicity of not having to look at two of them, Colonel Olson was working off of Colonel Stankowski's outlook calendar.

I was their executive officer, so a large portion of my job was to de-conflict the following day's calendar the night before, and nudge them along to where they were supposed to be. That Monday morning, I had a break in the schedule, so I thought I'd look at the Colonels' schedules for tomorrow. I noticed that there was an appointment for one of the Colonels to visit with EMEDS (Expeditionary Medical Squadron) regarding his right foot. I hadn't seen the appointment previously. In my mind, the appointment had to be for Colonel Olson, because I had seen him limp while we walked to breakfast that morning. I checked in with him, to let him know that he would need to cancel the appointment because he would be in mid-air on his way to Elmendorf AFB, Alaska when the appointment was to occur. He claimed it wasn't for him, it was for Colonel Stankowski, who'd made the appointment that morning. Apparently they both had foot problems. At this deployed location, the Qatari Desert, it wasn't uncommon to twist an ankle or sprain a foot, due the uneven terrain and rocks.

The conversation somehow turned to the boredom factor of the doctors and dentists at our location. Apparently, they were not very busy with customers. So "not busy" that they were looking for stuff to do. That sent up a flag in my mind. You see, I'm a traditional Guardsman, and normally, I'm not eligible for the same care as the active duty folks. "Not eligible" probably isn't the best choice of phrases. Actually, they just frown on it because they don't want Guardsmen saving up their dental visits and boo-boos for the taxpayer's

the Qatar Edge

dime. I asked the Colonel if he thought they would have time for a Guardsman. He said, "Sure what do you need done?" I explained to him that I have no emergency, and I have no pain, I just have some things that could use some attention from a dentist and a doctor, and they are both completely unrelated. One of my teeth that had some previous work was coming apart on me, and it wouldn't be a bad idea to get it filed off, pulled, or re-capped. The Colonel pushed a little more, because he was curious what that had to do with a doctor. "Okay, but what do you need a doctor for?" "Well Sir, my wife and I were talking about me getting a vasectomy." He said, "No problem, they have lots of folks available out here, they even have a cancer surgeon. The primary guy is an orthopedic surgeon due to the nature of most injuries at this location."

I began thinking to myself, "Wow, I can get a tooth fixed, and surprise the wife by getting snipped out here in the desert. That might even increase her sex drive, knowing that I can't get her pregnant anymore." You see, we were raising three children already, and my wife was nervous about having more. She was approaching 35 at the time, and she was buying into the public scare that women have more complications after that age. The other issue was that we were, and continue to be, Catholics. A vasectomy was, and also continues to be, forbidden in our church's belief structure. Don't misunderstand our motives here. We love our children. If you have children of your own, in any number more than one, you may understand why more of them aren't in our plans. My wife didn't want to wind up like my childhood friend's mother, Joyce Jacobs who had nine children. Somebody needed to tell that woman, "It's a vagina, not a clown car."

I looked up the phone number for EMEDS on the base intranet site. A young female airman spoke with me about scheduling the two separate events. Omitting the fact that I was a guardsman was intentional. While deployed, I had an active duty ID card. She said the dentist took appointments, but the doctor just saw walk-ins, and then made the diagnosis before continuing. I explained to her that there was no diagnosis needed, I just wanted a vasectomy. I detected a slight chortle in her voice. She said, "Hold on a minute, the doctor is right here, I'll ask him." Hearty laughter and muffled giggling could be heard in the background before she returned to the phone. She said, "The doctor is an orthopedic surgeon. If it's not a foot, we don't want to see it." Can you see this bad joke re-emerging yet? I couldn't resist. "It's not a foot honey, but I can't bitch about a couple of inches." The other end of the line went completely silent, and I thought, "Oh crap, she's going to call social actions on me." Then I heard the audible inhale, confirming

the Qatar Edge

her understanding of the punch line, followed by a good healthy cackling. When she finally calmed herself, she took the appointment for me to see the dentist. It was the quickest appointment scheduling I'd had in my life. My appointment was scheduled for two days from the time that I made it. I'm not sure if the expedient manner in which it was scheduled was a result of their lack of customers or the airman's desire to see this funny guy on the other end of the phone, who could make her laugh like that before her morning coffee. I later learned that the EMEDS girls had a sense of humor all their own. The base free-condom supply sat on their front desk. Every time they'd open a new box, they divided it into five randomly labeled baskets marked XL, Large, Medium, Small, and XSmall just to see who would take condoms from which basket.

Two days later, I went through a rough visit with the deployed dentist, Dr. Risk (not kidding). He and his lab tech discovered that my crumbling tooth was a symptom of a poorly done root canal 20 years ago by a Navy dentist. Additionally, there was some minor infection setting in. Dr. Risk informed me that he wanted to remove the remaining dental work, including the post, treat the infection, repack it, and basically perform a new root canal over two visits.

The lab tech's lack of skill with the x-ray machine reminded me of my father's desire to learn keyboard shortcuts way back when he was first learning to use a mouse. Like my father's cursed cursor moving in the exact opposite direction of the mouse because the mouse was tail-down instead of up, the lab tech kept moving the camera and the device that was in my mouth in the exact opposite direction he needed. Of course, I had half the toolbox and a rubber dam in my mouth as well. I couldn't swallow, so I was drooling worse than I did when Patricia Arquette humped Christian Slater in *True Romance*. Just as I could hear my drool slather the tarp covered floor, the lab tech said, "Hey, aren't you the guy that wanted a vasectomy?" Under the circumstances, I couldn't speak very well either. You try to have a conversation with a mouth full of dental instruments. I just lied, shaking my head left to right, hoping he'd accept that answer.

...and if I'm wrong, I'll always wish that I wasn't.

- Tony Shimley

I'd Walk Nine Miles for a Harmonica

It was Jim Burton's fortieth birthday. Burton, who went by Steve Canyon to strangers he had no intention of becoming too familiar with, was my hook-up for flags. He was a WSO (Weapon Systems Officer) on the F-15E Strike Eagle. The popular thing to do was to have an American flag flown over Iraq so you could present it with a certificate to your supporters back home. Burton would stuff his cargo pockets with folded flags on almost every sortie, just to keep up with demands. For him, we scoured the streets and alleys of downtown Doha, Qatar for a musical instrument he could purchase for his children. Children were the topic of a great deal of our conversation that day. One conversation that I hope I learned the most from involved the discipline of a potty-mouthed 12-year old girl.

Joey D. Ossian

Joining Jim and I on this day were Tony Shimley and Tom Edwards. It would probably be more accurate to state that I was joining them. Tony and Jim knew each other from an Air Force Base in Korea. Tony and Tom knew each other because they are both bomb loaders. Another Tom, Dr. Tom Osbourne, currently a congressman, and former Nebraska Husker football coach, probably wouldn't approve of me talking to this Colorado native and fan, but we both have R. Lee Irmey say "What's your name, Scumbag?" on our incoming email alerts, and we both know that eating too much black licorice makes your shit green, making us both true black licorice lovers. You have to like a guy that you have that much in common with. I mean, with those two common peculiarities, we could have been separated at birth. On the way to town, Tom Edwards was working on his "seven-level" (skill achievement level) with the Rio Riot, a portable juke box, wisely brought along by Tony Shimley, with hundreds of songs from the last three decades of popular music.

Between noon and 1600, all the locals head to the mosques to pray, closing all the small shops. We headed off to the local Starbucks for an 18 riyal caramel frappuchino. The major mall, City Center Mall, had open shops, so we began to search for our favorite. Tony Shimley and I had been to a shop previously, but were beginning to admit

the Qatar Edge

to ourselves that we'd never find it again with out some assistance. Each floor of the mall had a floor plan where you could find the store you were looking for, but we didn't know the name of the place. We couldn't even remember what floor it was on. Tony thought that by association we could assist in our search. We knew what it was next to, so we could find that to help us locate the "knife store." A previous co-worker was always checking out the carpets across the way from it, so we began looking for carpet shops. When the Mustafawi Exhibition showed up as a sporting goods store across from the carpets, Tony bet me a Diet Coke that the place was what we were looking for. It's not that I thought he was wrong; in fact, I wanted him to be right. Tony had lost three "Diet Coke bets" in a row to me, and I was hoping to end my winning streak, just to make him feel better. That sounds goofy, so I'll explain briefly the importance of a Diet Coke bet in Al Udeid. When you lose a Diet Coke bet, you don't just owe the competition a Diet Coke. The beverage had to be delivered to the winner's immediate location whenever he was thirsty. All he had to do was reach you by phone, and demand delivery. It turned out he was right, and we window shopped for the umpteenth time. Tony began to talk about his guilt, always keeping the proprietor busy, but never leaving any currency behind. For no better reason than that, we both negotiated a low bargain price for the Swiss Army Card. After a quick bite, and a check of our watches, we returned to our vehicle, anticipating that the shop vendors would be through with their ritual prayer.

"I'll shit a Christmas tree with lights if Achmed's House of Harmonicas is around that corner," claimed Shimley, after being misdirected again. Every local we asked for directions told us to go to the Softel Hotel, second floor. We never did find a music store in this location, but we are sure it's there. Either that, or the locals were having fun with us.

Jim had no healthy sense of paranoia as Tom and I did. It probably had something to do with the "fearless fighter" attitude. Approaching yet another alley, I handed Tom my spare six-inch Gerber E-Z out. It made us both feel better. We didn't think that Achmed would pull out an oozy, but we still felt better.

We finally found a Yamaha store, and Jim wound up buying a made-in-Japan instrument that resembled a double wood block tube device with a washboard installed. Every elementary school in the free world had one, but Jim thought his was special. And I thought all this time we were looking for something you could only get in Qatar. We humored Burton by letting him think we enjoyed and were amused by his constant attempts to fit his instrument into the currently playing juke-box tune. Tom would have been awarded his seven-level if he could have found more music on the Rio Riot that Jim could not play.

We can rebuild him . . .
We have the technology . . .

Mama Always Said I'd Go Blind

Thursday evening, January 8th, I had volunteered to call numbers for Bingo night, because the special services folks were short-handed. Many years ago, I worked at a Bingo parlor, so I was very familiar with the tempo of a good caller, and the clarity with which they must speak. It wasn't the first time I volunteered to call numbers, but it would certainly be the last time at Camp Andy.

This writing began on January 10, on the ride to Doha to see the Eye Cutter (Ophthalmologist) at Al Hamad Hospital in downtown Doha, Qatar. It was a little more than ironic that I could potentially get my eye cut on in Qatar (cutter). To this day, I don't know how it all happened. It is suspected that the damage was caused by the windstorms and the dry conditions the desert environment provided. I was reading perfectly as I called Bingo the night before.

the Qatar Edge

I woke up January 9th, 2004, and couldn't see shit out of my right eye. My first thought was that the sandman slit his bag and accidentally gave me too much sand. It has happened before. I'd just go to the Cadillac and rinse it out. Continued rinsing didn't help, so I got ready for work, planning to drive over to flight meds, which was adjacent to my work trailer. In hindsight, I probably couldn't see well enough to drive, but I did anyway. At this point, I still thought I had something in my eye, so I drove with limited depth perception to the EMXG (Expeditionary Maintenance Group), thinking "Mama always said I'd go blind if I didn't stop playing with that thing." I got to work and told my co-workers that I was walking over to flight medicine to get checked out. I met Hottie McYum, SSgt type, one each. Nobody ever made a DCU flight suit look that edible. As Tom Edwards would say, "She was hotter than two field mice fuckin' in a paint can." SSgt McYum claimed they didn't have the equipment at their location to properly look into my eyes, but volunteered to drive me over to Camp Andy where they would have such an apparatus. A young, tall, red-headed Captain, named Cory Harrison checked me out. Back home Dr. Harrison is an emergency room doctor, so in Camp Andy, he was the closest thing to an ophthalmologist. The Doc was very considerate, and pointed out that he had just brushed his teeth, so his breath should smell acceptable.

Unfortunately, my eye test was bad. Initial eye chart tests were coming in at about 20/200 in the right eye, while the left eye was my better-than-normal 20/15. After multiple questions, he made an appointment for me the following day, Saturday, at the Al Hamad Hospital in downtown Doha. So with nothing better to do, I went back to work.

That Friday afternoon I ran into Captain Harrison at the gym in Camp Andy. He said he could rule out a virus being the problem with my eye, and had narrowed it down to three possibilities: a detached retina, a dislocated lens, or some object resting on the retinal artery or nerve. He had never seen anything like it. Then he said, "It's like instant cataracts."

Friday night was movie night, and this Friday, the 9th of January, was no different. We watched *Tears of the Sun* with Bruce Willis. When I watched him get his right eye injured at the ending, I prayed it wouldn't be a bad omen.

Saturday morning at Al Hamad Hospital, Dr. Achmed Ishkabibble (ok, that's not his real name) dilated my eyes and checked me out with a strange contraption. I think he called the machine a slit-light scope, and he used it to see into my eye through my eye. Then he performed what he called an eye pressure test. I sat in front of another machine, and it shot little puffs of air into my eye. I still don't know what the heck he did that for, and it was more than a little irritating. I couldn't imagine an American ophthalmologist doing that, but then again, it was my first trip to any real eye doctor. He claimed that I had a cataract, but wouldn't do anything more about it until he had approval to operate from the American clinic at Al Udeid, where I was stationed.

The return to the clinic on base didn't help things much. Captain Harrison gave me multiple choices to think about, because he didn't want me to jump into cataract surgery without a second opinion. That second opinion would have to take place at Landstuhl Regional Medical Center in Ramstein, Germany. It was decided to get me on the next med-evac plane out of the AOR (area of responsibility).

Joey D. Ossian

**Chief Shimley and I making light
of my pending eye surgery.**

The first thing I did at that point was contact my friends in Ramstein. A year prior to this deployment, I attended BCOT (Basic Communications and Information Management Training) in Biloxi, Mississippi, at Keesler Air

the Qatar Edge

Force Base. Eight of my classmates were to be stationed at Ramstein Germany, so I had to let them know I was coming. Email was on the way.

Captain Susie Chun, a nurse at the EMEDS in Camp Andy, anti-hijacked (inspected) my bags for the C-130 flight, and on January 13th, 2004, I was landing at Kuwait City International Airport, to stay over night at Camp Wolverine/Wolf. When I checked into the hospital at Camp Wolverine, I met my medical technician, Senior Airman Allison Fieseler. Even with one eye, I could see she had beautiful hazel eyes. She would be my primary care-giver during my short stay. Senior Airman Fieseler told me that the majority of the base was Army, and had a high density of medical transients. I stayed in a squad-bay area, and when I checked in just before 1400 hours, I was the only patient on the ward.

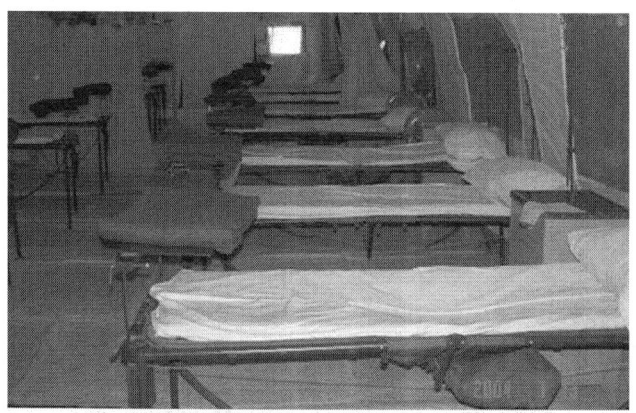

The patient ward at Camp Wolverine in Kuwait.

Joey D. Ossian

Camp Wolverine had to be the most boring place in the world. For starters, I had nothing to do but read, take pictures, flirt with "hazel eyes," and walk around the base to get familiar with it. With that in mind, I thought to myself. Okay, I'd read, but I haven't adjusted to reading with one eye yet. I'd walk around and take photos, but it had rained in Kuwait for about a week straight, and everything in sight was mud. As my good friend Mike Jepsen would say, "It was raining harder than a three-cunted caribou pissing off a bamboo bridge." I could familiarize myself with the base, but that would do no good, as I was departing at 0-dark-30 in the morning. Suddenly, it came to me. Find the BX, and shop! I got directions and found the BX. I wasn't the only one thinking this way. With nothing else to do on base, there was a line to get in. Once inside, I found a black t-shirt and a mesh tank-top labeled Camp Wolverine that I couldn't live without, a few chocolate Power Bars, paid and left. That task complete, and only half an hour burned, I looked for the D-Fac (Dining Facility) to sample the local cuisine. Then I remembered, the only thing worse than Air Force chow is Army chow. I'll never figure out why, but of all the military dining facilities I have entered, the Marines have the best chow halls in the entire set. That gruesome sustenance task accomplished, and another half hour burned, I walked back to the clinic.

the Qatar Edge

Posing in front of the Paradise Sands USO Club at Camp Wolverine, Kuwait.

It wasn't morning, but I woke up to get on another plane for the trip to Ramstein, Germany. That Wednesday morning, the 14th of January, I landed and took a bus to the LRMC (Landstuhl Regional Medical Center). I had an appointment that morning to see the ophthalmologist, Major Christopher Allen. Everybody on his schedule would get bumped by anybody in DCUs (Desert Camouflage Uniform). I felt like the President's son, getting seen immediately.

Dr. Allen determined that I had a posterior sub-capsar (inside the rear wall of the lens) cataract. Regardless of whether I noticed it prior to the morning of the 9th of January or not, his diagnosis was cataract. I didn't know prior to this experience, so I'll explain in layman's terms for my group of ignorant people. Cataracts develop over time. Imagine filling a glass of water, one drop at a time, one drop a day, over years. The visual distortion resulting from cataracts take time. Even the most rapid on-set takes months, and no case has been documented as happening over night. Dr. Allen says I just didn't notice. Trust me, I don't want to be special if it takes medical anomalies to accomplish it, but I'm certain that I would have noticed. I didn't. After all, I'm a shooter, and I frequently pick up elongated objects and sight-in on stuff, much like a practiced pool shooter checks his cues. I'm certain I had done it multiple times in the past week, because I do it everyday. Does that mean I'm right? Damn right it does!

Dr. Allen only did cataract surgery on Thursdays, and the following day was already full of other folks wearing DCUs, so I was scheduled to have the operation on Thursday, the 22nd of January. I had a week to wait. The anxiety of not knowing how the surgery would go, and if it would be successful was close to the worst anxiety I'd ever felt. My thoughts ranged from being able to stay in the military and shooting on the Nebraska National Guard Marksmanship Team to what disease did I have spreading to the other eye?

After the first appointment and diagnosis, I was on another bus to my new home at Kleber, a nearby Army Base. While there, I met the King of Kleber, Joe Wolf. Joe was one of the orderlies assigned to the unit's orderly room. Soon after we met, he assigned himself to provide me with nightly entertainment.

I lived in the Medical Transient Barracks, building 3210, for the next two weeks, under the scrutiny of the Army rules: 2200 bed checks and 0600 formations. To ease things a bit, the shirt (1st Sergeant) told me that officers weren't held accountable for the 2200 bed checks, and I was able to get out with Joe or my BCOT friends a couple times for Schnitzel and German beers.

A view from my window at the Medical Transient Company.

The night of the snow and ice storm in James Moyer's Beemer is a story in itself, which I'll get to shortly.

The procedure that Dr. Allen would have to perform involved the surgical pulverizing and removal of my affected lens with micro-tools inserted through a self-sealing incision in my right eye. With my lens removed, the second portion of the procedure would begin, by inserting an artificial plastic lens, model CC4204BF, serial number A1159875, through another self-sealing incision opposite the first. I had to stay over-night following the surgery, and when I woke, Dr. Allen removed the bandages. A day after the procedure, I tested 20/30, and the Doc said, I might even make it back to 20/15. The only thing I wouldn't get back would be the ability to focus very close, like reading from less than 18 inches away, or long distance clarity, beyond about 100 yards. I thought, shit! Two of my three favorite things to do will be impacted. I love to read, and I shoot in marksmanship competitions, mostly over 200 yards. I guess reading glasses are in my future, and also, practicing with my new dominant left eye for long-distance shooting competitions.

Four days after the surgery, on the 26th of January, I was hanging out with James Moyer on a Monday night. James is a young Lieutenant in the Comm field stationed at Vogelweh, just minutes from the LRMC. He is a proud Notre Dame graduate, and when it comes to his friends, one of the most ferociously protective, the Air Force will ever see. James and I met in November, 2002, when we were both assigned to BCOT class 021120, at Keesler Air Force Base. I'm old enough for James to be my Prom mistake, but my sense of humor and spontaneous-party attitude lured him in anyway.

the Qatar Edge

James picked me up at 1900 hours at Kleber. We finally got to dinner at Bristo-Maxi's in Ramstein village after a couple failed Euro-procurement attempts at ATMs. We'd made plans to meet two other BCOT classmates, but got stood up. One of them had a new girlfriend who I later learned, almost broke her nose that afternoon, and the other couldn't get a kitchen-pass from his wife. I'd been on alcohol rations for two months in the desert, so the two half-liters of Hefe-veisen with my Jager-schnitzel made everything funny.

The weather took a turn for the worse, as the four inches of snow began to get covered with about a quarter inch of ice. Watching the ice come down outside the window began to wear on James' nerves. At about 2130, we ventured out into the freezing rain. His '88 BMW cranked right up, but he began making excuses in anticipation of its near future performance, dooming it to fail soon. The summer slicks didn't grip the road too well, so with a slightly embarrassed tone, James asked me to climb my fat-ass into the back seat for assisted traction. He was hoping that the re-distribution of my 200 lbs. would put enough added force on the rear axle to help. It made a noticeable difference, but progressing slower than 90% of the traffic had James wishing out loud that he had four-wheel or at least, front-wheel drive. Then it happened. Going up the last hill to his house, we stopped moving. The wheels on the Beemer turned, but no progress was made. I got out to push, hoping my lack of weight in the back seat wouldn't be more than I could make up by pushing. Once I gave James enough momentum to take the hill, he got speed and got quite a distance away from me. I knew he'd eventually stop. At this point, the exhaustion and fumes were too much, and James decided our progress was far too minimal and too slow to warrant further effort. We were ready to give up, and crash at his buddy Orus's house at the bottom of the hill. We got turned around and prepared to head back down. The Beemer didn't quite have the turning radius to avoid the curb, so James naturally put the car in reverse to straighten out and have another go. That's when it hit him. Driving backwards effectively gave him "front-wheel drive" so to speak, since the driving wheels would now be leading the car. Again, I hopped in the back seat, shoving the coolant bottles out of the way, so there would be some weight over the "front wheels." Now, more determined than ever, James concentrated on backing his way home. The German Farmer with the tractor gave us a glimmer of additional hope despite the realization that he didn't speak English. James had been practicing his German enough to learn that the local farmer had no chain or other device used to tow vehicles. He was willing, however, to help push. Before beginning, he communicated to James, through a series of head signals that I should stand in the trunk for added weight above the driving wheels. We drove forward, down the hill about fifty yards to a bus stop loop so we could gain some momentum, and as we came back around, the German farmer joined me sitting in the trunk. Between me and that fat-ass German, we had almost 500 lbs. on the rear axle, giving James much traction, but little steering ability, due to the lack of tire contact on the other end of the vehicle. One more fat farmer, and we'd be doing wheelies. At the rate of about 100 feet per minute, me and the German bouncing the Beemer like a pimp-mobile to get it off the curbs and for more traction, we finally crested the hill. During the entire ride in the open trunk, the German farmer spoke to me in German. He could have been speaking in Uranus or out of his anus for all it mattered, because I had no clue what the hell he was saying. He just kept smiling and laughing, so I laughed along with him.

Joey D. Ossian

My laughter was genuine because the entire situation was funnier than shit. When his speaking finally gave that universal "questioning" tone, I fessed up. "I don't speak German." He just laughed some more. When he jumped off the trunk and waved goodbye, James gave his best learned German phrase about offering him a beer, but it was turned down as he went back to his tractor, now half a mile down the hill from our present location.

On level ground, I got back in the front seat with James and he was sweating! I guess the stress from the last hour was more of a work-out than my pushing him up the hill in the blasting wind. Our relatively level drive remaining to his house was filled with laughs, harder than we'd laughed in months. We shared our perspective of what had just happened, including talk of having a few beers over a *Family Guy* episode or two. Once inside, exhaustion took over, and we were soon giving in to the rather large sleep monsters that had climbed our backs.

Broken Wings

Dutch had taken over my duties during the two weeks I was in Germany. For the most part, this would have been an easy task. Under normal circumstances, it wouldn't have taken much effort to do both jobs. Unfortunately for Dutch, my departure in the second week of January meant he would be preparing for the Colonel's promotion ceremony mostly on his own. Lieutenant Colonel David P. Olson was going to make Colonel on February 1st, and Dutch was in charge of pulling it off. Prior to my departure, all I had done was contact the POCs (points of contact). Dutch would have to meet with comm, protocol, special services, crew chiefs, etc… He wasn't a happy man, and he initially aimed his frustrations at me. Dutch finally realized that once he assigned the tasks, all he had to do was monitor and make sure things were happening. When he realized that I'd return on the 28th of January, a few days prior to the ceremony, he breathed a huge sigh of relief. Dutch's relief was short-lived. Colonel Stankowski decided it would be a unique experience for Dutch to finish up, and just have me assist. The Colonel's thinking was that it wouldn't be fair to Dutch to have brought things this far, and not get the credit for seeing it through. I couldn't have agreed more.

The ceremony was scheduled for January 31st, in the afternoon. The Colonel was to be promoted under the F-15E Strike Eagle Sun Shades, right next to the maintenance trailers. General Egginton and Colonel Stankowski were going to pin on the eagles.

Prior to lunch, things were going as planned. Dutch and I went to pick up the cake at the dining facility. Loading the cake into the pickup is where the trouble started. It was a huge cake with colorful frosting. We couldn't get the door open far enough, and Dutch bumped the edge of the cake pan on the door, causing it to stop, while he was still going forward. Minor damage to the cake, major damage to the DCU (desert camouflage uniform). Imagine a baby blue glob of frosting smeared across the shoulder of a light sand colored fabric. We couldn't worry about that at the moment, the uniform would wash. A wash cloth, and a little bit of elbow grease helped enough that he didn't have to change.

Setting up the flags wasn't the hard part. Keeping them standing up straight proved to be a challenge, even with sand

the Qatar Edge

bags. I already spoke of the sandstorms and sudden breezes in the desert. We were running out of time when we heard the crash. Turning around to see what it was made me wish I hadn't. The American flag had hit the ground! Worse, the eagle on top of the pole lay on the ground with one of the wings tumbling away in wind. Dutch placed the broken wing in his cargo pocket, set the pole back up, and put four sand bags around the base before anybody even saw what happened. We'd perform the proper ceremony to replace the flag later, and order a new eagle. At that moment, there wasn't time. The ceremony was to start in ten minutes and the crowd would start to get in formation any minute.

The actual ceremony was flawless. Dutch and I stood next to the F-15E, behind and to the left of the podium, where each speaker would take their turn. During the entire event, all Dutch and I could think of was the busted wing. Well, I'm sure Dutch was also thinking about the pretty blue stripe adorning his shoulder. Nobody ever asked about the wing, but if you look closely, you can see it in darn near every photo taken that day.

Lt Ossian posing on the F-15E Strike Eagle. Notice the one-winged Eagle on top of the American Flag.

Head Gear

What we wore on our heads shouldn't have been such a huge deal in the desert. You'd think that everyone would just wear a DCU boonie so they wouldn't burn their ears off. The base commander took a page from Marine Corps history and decided that if nobody wanted to screw with the Marines, he'd authorize the eight-point Marine style hat, or cover, as we Marines call it. His theory was that if the enemy thought we were all Marines, they'd leave us the hell alone. Even the prior service Marines were torn about the idea. We wanted them because we rated them, but we didn't want everybody else to have them, because they didn't. Then I was told that there was a shortage of the cover, and only the permanent party personnel were going to get them issued. Imagine me, a prior service Marine, seeing a bunch of Air Force guys wearing my cover when I can't. I wasn't taking it lying down. I went on-line and found a website where I could order my own damn cover. I spoke with my co-workers and friends to see who else wanted in on the order, and I wound up ordering six.

Waiting for the order to come brought some interesting events with impact. After the first week passed, Chief Shimley walked into the building wearing an eight-point Marine style cover. We both knew you weren't supposed to wear hats or covers indoors, he just wanted to make sure I saw that he had one before me. It worked. I was pissed. My face was set, and I glared at him, fighting the grin that was spreading across my face. "I see how you are. You gonna just stand there sporting the new duds, or are you going to tell me where you got it, and where mine is?" "They wouldn't let me have more than one, but you might be able to go to the Desert Depot (supply) and get yourself one."

Chief tossed me the keys, and I was on my way to supply. I began to think to myself, Chief was permanent party, that's how he got the cover. I'm going to have to lie or come up with something. I know! They are girls, I'll schmooz! As plainly as I could, I walked in to the Desert Depot, looked both the counter girls right in the eye, and asked, "What's a Marine got to do to get an eight-point Marine style cover?" "Talk to the boss." They pointed to an office door, so I knocked, was invited in by a male voice, and repeated my question. "What's a Marine got to do to get an eight-point

the Qatar Edge

Marine style cover?" "Prove it." I showed him my Marine Corps ring and an Eagle, Globe, and Anchor tattoo, and he asked me what size I wanted. That was simple. Good thing the counter girls didn't ask me to prove it, I might have gotten into trouble.

Two weeks later, the covers came in. I spoke with the remaining folks who were in with me. Chief already had his, but offered to buy one if I couldn't sell them. Dutch didn't have one yet, but wasn't sure he wanted one. He'd heard that there was a shipment coming in, and that he could possibly get one for free in another week. Tom was anxiously awaiting his, and paid promptly. Since the Desert Depot so kindly parted with one for me two weeks ago, I had five spare covers to sell. I put the word out on the base "chat" bulletin board. Multiple phone calls and emails came in immediately to reserve a cover. They were gone in two hours! I sold them for $10 a piece. The price tag on the hats was about $8 per hat, plus tax and shipping, bringing the total to $59.64. Selling the hats netted me 36 cents, or six cents a hat (Glad I wasn't in it for the money). What the buyers didn't know was that my shipment beat the big delivery by days. The entire base could get them for free just a couple weeks later. I'm glad I didn't get stuck with all six of them.

Choke Yourself!

Thursday the 19th of February, 2004

We would plan Thursday nights as soon as the last Thursday was over. It was the highlight of the week outside of The Shield. Around the workouts, we'd schedule someone to get there an hour early to save seats and order pizza. Shimley always ordered the spicy "light-it-up" pizza, and "paid" for it the next day if you know what I mean. Every routine was an event. The required potty breaks, fetching more beers, watching each other's bingo cards, harassing the bad bingos. A bad bingo is when someone calls "Bingo" when they don't really have it. We even got to the point where we'd predict "bad bingo" on the rookies or when we knew that not enough numbers were called in the right rows. Tom and the Chief were always there. James Wine, and the Shirt (First Sergeant), Mark Campbell, joined us often. Dutch, Dave, Kat, LL, and whoever they invited rounded out our group. Nobody from our group ever won anything. The prizes were mostly electronic goods that the special services folks had purchased from customer contributions. Unfortunately, all our group ever did was contribute. Most of the fun became harassing "bad bingo." The crowd would wait in anticipation when a staff member was checking the validity of a bingo. If it was bad, and it frequently was, our group would yell "Choke Yourself!" like R. Lee Irmey did to Private Pyle in *Full Metal Jacket*. I don't know why, I guess that was our chosen humorous punishment.

Tom Edwards and Tony Shimley at the Wheel for Bingo Night.

Even when circumstances made it likely that a good bingo was just called, we'd yell anyway.

Joey D. Ossian

Dave and I were sitting next to each other this Bingo night, across from Tom and Tony at the end of a row formed by about four tables. Since we were both into collecting and trading military unit coins, and had recently "awarded" each other with coins from our respective units, he coined me. An explanation is required here for the non-military. When you are "coined" it is a challenge to see if you are carrying the coin. The rules are simple. When someone coins you, they do so by producing a replica of the coin they have awarded you. If you can produce the coin on demand, they owe you a beverage of choice. If you cannot, you must respond by offering to purchase their beverage. I had a copy of the coin Dave challenged with, so he was buying. As I got up, Chief Shimley offered to watch my bingo card.

Dave and I returned after waiting in a long line for the second of our three-drink limit. Chief was acting peculiar, and I soon discovered that my card was "one away" under the Chief's watchful eye. He had my card down to waiting on only "N31" to be called. I sat down and it was the next number called. I sounded off "BINGO" as loud as I could, I was so pumped. I was one of three bingos and all I was thinking was please be a cash prize so we can split it. If it was a normal prize, we would have to draw cards to determine the winner.

the Qatar Edge

The gal verifying cards told me she didn't call G53. I couldn't believe it. G53 was one of the spaces marked on my card. I called BAD BINGO! I thought, maybe I can slink away and nobody will know I had a bad bingo. There were two others still being verified – I tried to get away, and man did I get razzed! I was thinking, Chief, you suck! I got back to the table and he wasn't even there. Campbell and Wine were laughing at me, talking about how Chief set me up. Chief returned and I was ready to catch hell and give it back for how he did me. He was as surprised as me. Chief didn't set me up, he really thought he played it right and might get to split with me, since he did all the work. I explained the problem and how I thought he must have been laughing his ass off when I hollered and went to collect. Chief continued to profess his innocence. Then it sort of became a joke, Chief offering to watch other's cards. He proved his loyalty and gave me the payback opportunity a few games later, by asking me to watch his card. The last game of the night – the blackout, for the jackpot of $400+ dollars. I honestly hoped he'd win while he was gone, just to prove to him that I wasn't upset and that I wouldn't bust his chops. "Now's your chance LT" I kept hearing. Chief's card sucked – he didn't get a damn number out of the first ten called. Hell, it looked like I wasn't even watching it, and I began to worry that he'd think so too. By the time he came back, of the 25 spots on the card, he had free and about six more. My card only had four left to cover. He gave me a funny look as if he didn't understand and as if I were guilty of something. I felt like crap with Chief looking at me like that, but I told him honest, "Chief, your card just sucked this game." I should have said, "Payback's a bitch."

Field UAs

All branches of the military are tested randomly for drug use and in all cases that I've heard, there is zero tolerance. The "Whiz Quiz" isn't something you can study for, but it is something you can fail or pass. The member is required to fill a cup, not terribly unlike a Dixie, with urine, while a senior trusted member observes the urine leaving the body and traveling into the cup. The urine is then analyzed (urinalysis) or tested to see if the member is using illegal drugs or controlled substances.

To my knowledge, nobody deployed to Al Udeid Air Base was expected to test. Either the clinic expected the 6,000 of us to have some honor and integrity plus under these austere conditions, or they were planning on being too busy and without the proper equipment. I suspect the latter. Nobody knew this would be the case, and we had some "newbees" to initiate, so the wheels started spinning.

Cory Shipp was new to Al Udeid and had less than a year in the USAF. Dutch Umbaugh and I decided we would have a little fun. Cory was a great kid, but we gave him a ton of crap because every time he opened the office, the TV would find its way to the Sesame Street channel. We recruited the other airman from the office, Gabe "Sensuous" Sirlopu to help us play the prank. Gabe picked up the nickname "Sensuous" because he was so lazy, every time he wanted something from the fridge, he'd wait for someone else to get up first. He'd say, "Since you was (sounding like sensuous) up…" Gabe's role was easy. All he had to do was play along, and act like he didn't know anything was up.

Being the Executive Officer for the Maintenance Group, I was the boss of the office. Dutch was my right-hand man, and he and I ironed out a plan. With a perfectly straight face, I strolled into the room and informed Technical Sergeant Dutch Umbaugh that we'd been tasked with field UAs, and that he had to watch the airman in the office, Gabe and Cory, pee in a cup. He groaned and complained something about watching little pricks and waiting for the stage fright to wear off. SRA (Senior Airman) Gabriel Sirlopu was in on the joke, so Dutch called him to the head first. Cory stayed back in the office while Gabe carefully filled his clear Dixie with apple juice instead of urine. The head (bathroom) had a row of sinks with white plastic ledges for shaving

the Qatar Edge

gear. Gabe set his cup on the ledge with a grin on his face. He knew he wouldn't get to watch, but he was laughing because he knew what would probably happen. Cory was brought in, and then directed to fill his cup and leave it on the ledge next to the other. This is when I entered. Cory set his cup on the ledge, and then he and Dutch turned questioningly to me. Dutch said, "Where's the kit?" There was no such thing as a UA field test kit, but I replied, "We couldn't get one, you'll have to do the sip-check." "No way, I ain't sippin' piss again, you do it." "I'm the L-T, and I've sipped my share. I'm giving you a direct order." "Shit LT, I forgot to have them label their cups." "I guess you'll have to temp check them as well." "You got a thermometer?" "Come on Dutch, you're going to sip them both, you got a problem dipping your finger too?" "Oh, man!" Dutch and I both knew that temperature wasn't taken, even on real UAs, but he explained to Cory that to identify whose urine was whose, temperature had to be taken, and the cooler one would be the first one completed, or the one that had time to sit and cool off a bit. Dutch recalled which one was which, a big key to not having this trick backfire on you, and he cautiously dipped his index finger into the apple juice. He then convincingly made a disgusted face. "This one has to be Gabe's, cause it ain't even warm no more, and that other one's steaming." "Is that one yours, Cory?" I said, pointing to the one still steaming. "Yes Sir." "Okay, I guess you don't have to temp check the other. Which sample belongs to who is settled." "You ready for the sip-check, Dutch?" "Yes Sir." "Have you eaten the crackers to cleanse your palette?" "Don't need to, haven't had nothing since breakfast." That's when Corey couldn't take it anymore. "Hey man, he ain't really going to sip that piss, is he? What does he do that for?" I said, "Don't worry, it's sterile. TSgt Umbaugh has been trained to taste sweet, sour, tart, and other shit to tell if there is anything in it. He'll know if there is a need for further testing." Dutch picked up the cup of apple juice, and the room fell silent. I knew it was juice, but set my face firm, pretending to be into the science of it all. Corey had the most disgusted look on his face, but silently watched as Dutch slowly brought the cup to his lips. Dutch poured half the cup into his mouth, and swished it around with a thoughtful look on his face. "Tastes sort of sweet…..really not bad." Then, much to Corey's surprise, Dutch tossed the other half cup into his mouth and swallowed. Corey ran into the nearest stall, and began heaving his breakfast into the stool, hoping he was never tasked to "field-test" his future airman's urine samples.

My theory on why Priests tend to be homosexuals,
as explained to Father Jose Del Toro:

Just to clarify things here, I don't really think Catholic Priests have a tremendous tendency to be queerer than their parishioners. In fact, I have friends who are Catholic Priests. I simply enjoy stirring the pot.

Captain (Father/Chaplain) Jose Del Toro replaced Captain Terry Fox as the 379th Expeditionary Maintenance Group Chaplain shortly after Christmas. Father Del Toro was an interesting man to say the least. He knew his religion, but he was fairly ignorant when it came to the military and its aircraft. For starters, he thought all the external fuel tanks were bombs (an easy mistake), and secondly, he couldn't understand why you would want to retract landing gear, if you're just going to reset it to land again later. I guess the science of aerodynamics isn't part of theology. While Father Del Toro may not have been the representation of

Joey D. Ossian

Catholic Priests that sparked this theory, he was definitely open enough to weird conversation that you could razz him about it.

There has been a great deal of media exposure in the last few years regarding the Catholic Church and how a handful of its clerics have poorly represented the Church. Now I can't claim to know why this happens as many people do, but I do have a theory. The day after the Fire Department showed up, and Dutch put up his "Trogdor Burnination" sign because Father Del Toro tried to burn the trailer down by over-nuking the popcorn, I explained it to him like this:

There is a shortage of good Catholic Priests. Catholic churches and schools likely begin recruiting future priests when boys are young teenagers in junior high and high school. Now imagine that you are a boy between the ages of 14 and 18, and you are in a Catholic environment, be it a church organization or school. If you are approached by a nun, priest, or other leader in the church about the idea of pursuing the priesthood, you are likely to react in one of two ways: A boy is either interested, or dead set against it. This reaction is typically based on the boy's level of interest in one thing: girls.

It's a well known fact that priests aren't allowed to marry or have sex. Boys that like girls aren't likely to volunteer

the Qatar Edge

to give that up, especially when they are approaching the peak age of sexual interest and desire. It's the nature of our society (or at least it has been) to look down on homosexual tendencies, and a typical boy in a typical environment won't have many opportunities to explore those curiosities. In my mind, and this is a big key to the theory, a boy who has no interest in girls may not realize that he is interested in boys. I think this is because he may be subconsciously fighting off the feelings, because they are learned to be unacceptable. Therefore, a boy who is "wired differently" may see the priesthood as an option when his heterosexual classmates won't. With the priesthood as a remaining option, the pool from which to recruit priests will have a higher percentage of homosexuals.

Are there holes in this theory? Absolutely. Shoot it full. I can't prove anything. After all, who is going to track the boys from high school through their Catholic Priest careers? And then, how frequently will the offending priest tell you they didn't realize they were homosexuals when they were recruited? This isn't a theory to which the Catholic Church or any Priest is going to help bring validity.

Father Jose Del Toro had some good arguments though. He showed me statistics that showed other religions having higher incidents of infidelity, to include those denominations that allow marriage. His argument was that "World Religion" was out to get the Catholic Church, and that Catholics were the easiest target for the media. I still have to wonder, why don't we ever hear about priests abusing little girls?

Dry Camp

March 18th

Packed and waiting, 2Lt Molly Erickson (my replacement) said I must feel naked without a pocket knife on me. Molly and I first met in November of 2003 when she arrived in Biloxi, Mississippi for BCOT training a week after me. I had seen her recently in a food court on Ramstein Air Base, Germany just a few weeks back with a classmate, Tommy Marshall, from BCOT. In fact, she turned out to be the girlfriend who had almost broken her nose preventing Tommy from attending dinner with me and James Moyer. We had no idea we'd see each other again so soon. Molly's comment about feeling naked made me realize that I still had the Swiss card recently purchased at the Mustafawi Exhibition in my wallet. I'd get busted for sure by the metal detector. My options were to mail it home, try to sneak it on the plane, or find my bags and shove it into one of them.

Joey D. Ossian

I went back to the checked bag area to see if I could locate the bags, but they were gone, and another bin was in its place. I spoke with one of the airmen at the desk, and he gave me another airman who reluctantly walked me out to a row of bins, knowing I'd never find it. I was optimistic because my bags were at the top of the bin (marked NGU for Norfolk) I loaded them in, and I knew they were flagged with strips of red cloth from a shredded pair of my boxers. The flags caught my eye, and I successfully placed the offending sharp object in one of my bags. The things people will do for souvenirs.

Kat left two days ago, and Shimley's phone hasn't stopped ringing. Our final week together included a stop at the mall to go ice-skating, lunch at McDonalds, a hotel bar, and the Qatar Master's Golf Tournament. Toward the end, Tom and I snuck into the golf tournament where only media were allowed with a camera, and watched the winner on his final approach. Tiger wasn't there, but some decent big names were. The final week together brought tears to our eyes, some more than others, and we vowed to plan a reunion. We put Tom Edwards on the plane last night, and he promised to come see me in five years when the Colorado Buffaloes come to Lincoln's Memorial Stadium for some football. There are times in your life when being in the company of certain people makes you a better person. They become a part of you forever. It's rare that it happened this way, but we all realized it before our group parted.

Joey and Tom race down the slide at McDonald's in Doha, Qatar.

On this day, I sat and waited in the pax terminal for the call to load the plane. Chief Anthony Shimley and 2Lt Molly Erickson came by early, but Tony hates the tearful goodbye so he didn't want to hang around. Colonel Stankowski showed for cake and ice cream, spoke to me and a few other folks, and made a quick get away as well. The visits were over. I contemplated the wait, and the length of the trip home, my mind drifting off to future reunions and lessons learned.

I found out earlier in the day that an incident occurred last night, St Patrick's Day, at the Wagon Wheel. It caused the Big Egg (General Egginton) to ban alcohol sales from the base for the near future. Apparently two young airmen got drunk and misbehaved on the bus ride back to Coalition City.

A few days prior, this incident would never have happened. When people got drunk at the Wagon Wheel before, they stumbled home. The Wagon Wheel was in the center of Camp Andy. Camp Andy was the tent-city home to the entire base. The new club in Coalition City wasn't finished yet, so if you wanted entertainment, you continued to frequent the Wagon Wheel, and then you took the bus to your new home. If they had still lived in tent city, they could have stumbled back to their tents, and nobody would have been the wiser. Apparently, one of the airmen puked on the bus and his buddy tried to take over the driving duties during the driver swap-out.

I'm wondering who these airmen are and what impact the event will have on their careers and lives. Will that be their biggest mistake, or did they begin a pattern? Are they doomed to a pattern of minor incidents that will inevitably begin to pile up on them? Will their superiors begin to watch more carefully and start looking for ammunition? Perhaps my calling is counseling young offenders such as these, given my experience. Hopefully they'll stay away from the booze, out of trouble and out of the public eye. But then again, what fun would that be?

afterword

If I ended up at the end of my life having been an astronaut, but having sacrificed my family along the way or living my life in a way that didn't glorify God, then I would look back on it with great regret, and having become an astronaut would not really have mattered all that much.

- Rick Husband

Versions of the Truth

Somewhere along the way, I got really good at stretching the truth. Call it embellishment, call it fabrication, call it "little" or "white." It's a real skill, but I'm still telling lies. I know why the "Coalition for Morality" in the Air National Guard (ANG) wants me out. I don't know why it embarrasses me, I just didn't want other people to know. From their perspective, I make them look like normal people, instead of the "lily-white" version they want the public to see.

There are three versions circulating regarding my retirement or transfer. They all have some truths to them, but your relationship to me decided which version you heard: I could be looking for a new home because the Air Guard Surgeon General claims I'm a liability due to my new plastic lens in my right eye. I got this idea when I was told during a chapter two physical for the Army Guard that I'd need a waiver from an ophthalmologist that states I'm not a liability for further injury. That's the potential transfer or "medical discharge" version. It has some minor fabrications but the Coalition for Morality may use this one as an excuse. I'm looking at "upward mobility" was the story, if I spoke to you about a transfer to another state or the Army Reserve. "Nobody ever retires from the Air Guard." "How am I ever going to make Major?" There are lots of truths in this version as well. Those are the two versions, in order, that I told for quite a while. The third reason and real truth is, I pissed off the Coalition for Morality and I'm being pushed out. Potential transfers just to stay in the military are really what are keeping me from resisting at the moment. The threat right now is "board of separation" if I try to stay in the Air Guard.

Three things made the Coalition for Morality desire to end my Nebraska Air National Guard career. Actually, that's a little premature. As of this writing, I anticipate that it will be over soon, but I'm still hanging on by the skin of my teeth. By themselves, they weren't all that bad, but put together, there may be no room left for me.

Part one of this book details the summer of 2002, when there were allegations against me, claiming I kissed an 18 year old girl. In itself, the accusation isn't bad. You might think that it should just be an issue for my wife and me to discuss, but I was the student's high school principal at the time, so the papers had a good ol' fashioned Joey bashing.

Having resigned from that position gave me plenty of time to realize my dream in writing. I wrote and published a book that chronicled many of the silly things I did as a young Marine and Army Guardsman. *A Marine's Lapse in Synapse* was released in January of 2003. The language I inevitably had to use when speaking of the antics of young Marines ticked a few people off.

In my mind, those two events weren't bad or slanderous. After all, I didn't say anything bad about the President, or any branch of service, but it pissed off enough of the "higher-ups" that attention was drawn to me. Now they were gunning for Joey.

A deployment to Geilenkirchen, Germany during the last two weeks of March, 2003, gave them the ammunition they needed. It's a double standard. One of the recruiting attractions for the Air National Guard is the good times in over-seas locations. Then when you have a good time, you get ass deep in shit. I was told that the trip to "Girly-Licken" was a reward for me, because I went to BCOT for four months to fill a slot in the unit. I went with the mind set of having a great time. Prior to our departure from Lincoln, I spoke with many maintenance folks who had been to Geilenkirchen. The underlying theme of these conversations was "good times." Still, I knew I had a job to do, and tremendous responsibilities. The short trip didn't require a maintenance officer, the billet I filled, but there was an empty seat on the plane. Upon arrival, I requested to be housed in the same building as the maintenance folks. I wanted to live with those with whom I worked. Normally, officers wouldn't reside in the same location as the enlisted folks, but they made an exception for me. I was even allowed an enlisted roommate.

Other than the declaration of War on Terrorism in the middle of our trip, it was just what I expected: great times, lots of German beer and chocolate, lots of souvenirs, lots of sites to see. One event changed the outcome of our return, and remains the singular straw that "broke the camel's back."

Seven people from the maintenance package, including myself, ventured into Geilenkirchen one afternoon for a car show. We took one of the vans assigned to us. I was particularly excited about this trip because I felt close to all the people involved. I knew the afternoon would be relaxing and enjoyable.

Shortly after our arrival, we agreed to separate into two parties. I went with two enlisted troops, and the senior enlisted person took the remaining members with him. A mistake, fatal to my National Guard career, occurred at this moment. I didn't talk to the Senior Master Sergeant (SMSgt) about a plan to meet in case we happened to miss each other. Perhaps I didn't think about it, because the area we were in was about four-blocks square, with only two bars. Perhaps I dismissed it because he was a very experienced SMSgt, and he didn't mention it.

We missed each other for the rest of the afternoon. I suggested to my friends that we make a quick trip back to the van just to see if anyone was there waiting for us. The van was gone. All three of us assumed that the other party wasn't too worried about us, if they could bring themselves to leave. So my party decided to get a bite to eat and make the best of things until we caught a cab for the four-mile trip back to base that evening.

I never saw anybody so mad in my life. I was chewed a brand-new back side. I tried to explain to the SMSgt that he needed to share the responsibility with me for not discussing a plan to meet in the event we were separated. He didn't want to hear it. Several of you may be wondering why an officer would take an ass-chewing from an enlisted person. He was scared and venting, and I'm not the kind of officer who hides behind his rank. We calmly revisited things in the morning, and I was convinced that we had seen the end of the situation. I guess I forgot about CYA (cover your ass).

I got a rather large dose of back-stabbing upon our return to Lincoln. During the next drill, my group commander wanted to have a "come-to-Jesus" with me. During this meeting, the Colonel produced two copies of a typed sheet of paper containing a list of things I had allegedly done in Germany. There is no mystery to who put together this list. In fact, I was told by my Commander that the SMSgt on the trip had given it to him. The list ranged from "wearing boxers with things hanging out" and "farting in people's faces" to "waking people up in the middle of the night, looking for alcohol" and "pissing out windows in the middle of the night" (Okay, so I might have pissed out a window). What disturbed me most about the list was that the majority of the statements began with "A crew chief told me" or "somebody said," and that the Colonel was still reading. You don't hold water with a list of he said, she said, second hand fabrications.

The Colonel informed me that I needed to get "squeaky clean" and stay that way for quite some time, if I wanted to be considered for upward movement around here. He added that if I was one of his squadron commanders, I'd have been relieved. As a Lieutenant, you're allowed a few more mistakes. I didn't know how important this event would be to my career at the time. In fact, I didn't find out for quite some time that this new, entirely different snowball was rolling down the hill, and building up steam.

Thursday, May 6th, 2004

I received email from the Maintenance Group Commander (MXG/CC) asking for a face-to-face visit with me. The Colonel was and continues to be a valuable friend and mentor, so I made arrangements to meet with him immediately.

Friday, May 7th, 2004

The Colonel informed me that the Wing Commander had decided that my services were no longer required. His intention was to have me leave quietly. The Wing Commander would do this either by convincing me to retire, which I was eligible to do, or I could stay, forcing his hand to non-retain or hold a board of separation. It didn't look good. I contacted the Nebraska Army National Guard immediately, knowing that they were in desperate need of officers. I stayed at the All Ranks Club until they ran out of Captain Morgan, and called in sick to work the next morning.

It didn't matter that I spent the entire damn winter in the Persian Gulf collecting accolades. The Wing King wanted me gone. He was new, and I was part of his "Wing cleansing."

Is playing hard a bad thing? That depends on what your perspective of playing hard is. I've always said, "I work hard, and I play hard," but what the hell does that mean? I think most of us agree that to work hard means to show up everyday, do the job right, and earn the money. Does to "play hard" mean to do the same in your off duty time? Be intense, have fun, cause trouble? I don't think we all agree on what "play hard" means. The current health craze and TV media have a good-sized contingent leaning toward the active lifestyle to include: mountain biking, canoeing, and jumping out of planes. My peer group has generally considered "playing hard" to have a more derogatory meaning. We shut down clubs, talk shit, and chase whores. Not much of that activity results in cardiovascular activity, but it does get our blood pumping.

I guess I'm not the glowing lily-white example the Air Guard wants to represent them anymore. You know what they say about "one aw-shit?" Well, they want to pin four on me. The first three that I previously mentioned, and part II of the *Marine's Lapse in Synapse* series that came out in February of 2004.

Saturday, May 22nd, 2004

I was checking the email at home when I received word from my Group Commander that the Army National Guard was not going to accept my transfer. I had previously completed the necessary documentation, and the chapter two physical to move from the Air Guard back to the Army. Why leave the Air Guard? Well, it's not for the same reasons I left branches before. In the past, it was location and opportunity. I left the Marines at the end of my tour in 1987 for the Army Guard, because the Army Guard was in Lincoln (and I didn't know about the Air Guard). I left the Army and joined the Air Guard because I found out about the Air Guard. If I leave the Air Guard, it will be for a brand new reason. They don't want me anymore. I finally did enough stupid shit after 21-plus years that the decision, unanimously, was that I would be non-retained or separated. Diplomatically, that meant, I've lived out my usefulness to the Air National Guard. When the MXG/CC informed me that the ARNG didn't want me back, I realized that somebody with a lot of pull was waving red flags and blinking, big-red warning signs. Realization: I'm a dirt bag. I told myself that I wasn't done yet and that I'd call every recruiter in a five-state area to find out who didn't care. I was hopeful, but not holding my breath. I just didn't like the idea of somebody else telling me it was time to hang up the combat boots. Hell, I may even be willing to resign the commission and be enlisted again, just to stay in.

still here

I'm torn about ending this book. Most authors have trouble ending books because a month or two after publication, they always think of something they forgot to include, or something they wished they'd done differently. My reasons include those, but mostly I'm torn because the story isn't finished. I could sit around and wait until it's over, but if the Coalition for Morality waits long enough to see what I'm going to do, or if they "forget" to do something long enough, I could remain out of sight and out of mind for another ten years. If that turns out to be the case, I may write another book.

Lt Joey Ossian upon his return from The Persian Gulf, March 2004.

about the author

Joey Dean Ossian was born in Tecumseh, Nebraska, in September of 1964. He also graduated high school from there, but spent a good deal of time in between being moved around the Midwest by his father in his quest for the perfect school administrator position.

After four years in the Marine Corps, during his Nebraska National Guard days, Joey became an elementary teacher, and spent two years as a K-12 Principal before being deployed multiple times in support of Operation Enduring Freedom and Operation Iraqi Freedom.

Mr. Ossian still works with the National Guard, writes, and watches his children grow. Joey lives with his wife and three children near Columbus, Nebraska.

Printed in Great Britain
by Amazon.co.uk, Ltd.,
Marston Gate.